TECHNICAL COLLEGE OF THE LOWCOUNTRY
LEARNING RESOURCES CENTER
POST OFFICE BOX 1288
BEAUFORT, SOUTH CAROLINA 29901-1288

Furman
v. Georgia
Fairness and
the Death Penalty

FAMOUS
TRIALS

Titles in the Famous Trials series include:

Furman
v. Georgia
Fairness and the Death Penalty

by Bradley Steffens

Lucent Books, San Diego, CA

No part of this book may be reproduced or used in any form or by any means, electrical, mechanical, or otherwise, including, but not limited to, photocopy, recording, or any information storage and retrieval system, without prior written permission from the publisher.

Library of Congress Cataloging-in-Publication Data
Steffens, Bradley, 1956–
    Furman v. Georgia: fairness and the death penalty /
    by Bradley Steffens.
        p. cm. — (Famous trials)
    Includes bibliographical references and index.
    ISBN 1-56006-470-6
    1. Georgia—Trials, litigation, etc. 2. Furman, William
Henry—Trials, litigation, etc. 3. Capital punishment—
Georgia. 4. Capital punishment—United States [1. Capital
punishment. 2. Furman, William Henry—Trials, litigation, etc.
3. Trials.] I. Title. II. Series.
KF228.F87 M35 2001
345.73'0773—dc21
                                                    00-012112

TECHNICAL COLLEGE OF THE LOWCOUNTRY
LEARNING RESOURCES CENTER
POST OFFICE BOX 1288
BEAUFORT, SOUTH CAROLINA 29901-1288

Copyright © 2001 by Lucent Books, Inc.
P.O. Box 289011
San Diego, CA 92198-9011
Printed in the U.S.A.

Table of Contents

Foreword

"The law is not an end in and of itself, nor does it provide ends. It is preeminently a means to serve what we think is right."

William J. Brennan Jr.

THE CONCEPT OF JUSTICE AND THE RULE OF LAW are hallmarks of Western civilization, manifested perhaps most visibly in widely famous and dramatic court trials. These trials include such important and memorable personages as the ancient Greek philosopher Socrates, who was accused and convicted of corrupting the minds of his society's youth in 399 B.C.; the French maiden and military leader Joan of Arc, accused and convicted of heresy against the church in 1431; to former football star O.J. Simpson, acquitted of double murder in 1995. These and other well-known and controversial trials constitute the most public, and therefore most familiar, demonstrations of a Western legal tradition that dates back through the ages. Although no one is certain when the first law code appeared or when the first formal court trials were held, Babylonian ruler Hammurabi introduced the first known law code in about 1760 B.C. It remains unclear how this code was administered, and no records of specific trials have survived. What is clear, however, is that humans have always sought to govern behavior and define actions in terms of law.

Almost all societies have made laws and prosecuted people for going against those laws, but the question of which behaviors to sanction and which to censure has always been controversial and remains in flux. Some, such as Roman orator and legislator Cicero, argue that laws are simply applications of universal standards. Cicero believed that humanity would agree on what constituted illegal behavior and that human laws were a mere extension of natural laws. "True law is right reason in agreement with nature," he wrote,

6

world-wide in scope, unchanging, everlasting. . . . We
may not oppose or alter that law, we cannot abolish it, we
cannot be freed from its obligations by any legislature. . . .This [natural] law does not differ for Rome and
for Athens, for the present and for the future. . . . It is and
will be valid for all nations and all times.

Cicero's rather optimistic view has been contradicted
throughout history, however. For every law made to preserve
harmony and set universal standards of behavior, another has
been born of fear, prejudice, greed, desire for power, and a host
of other motives. History is replete with individuals defying and
fighting to change such laws—and even to topple governments
that dictate such laws. Abolitionists fought against slavery, civil
rights leaders fought for equal rights, millions throughout the
world have fought for independence—these constitute a mini-
mum of reasons for which people have sought to overturn laws
that they believed to be wrong or unjust. In opposition to Cicero,
then, many others, such as eighteenth-century English poet and
philosopher William Godwin, believe humans must be con-
stantly vigilant against bad laws. As Godwin said in 1793:

Laws we sometimes call the wisdom of our ancestors.
But this is a strange imposition. It was as frequently the
dictate of their passion, of timidity, jealousy, a monopo-
lizing spirit, and a lust of power that knew no bounds.
Are we not obliged perpetually to renew and remodel
this misnamed wisdom of our ancestors? To correct it by
a detection of their ignorance, and a censure of their
intolerance?

Lucent Books' *Famous Trials* series showcases trials that exem-
plify both society's praiseworthy condemnation of universally
unacceptable behavior, and its misguided persecution of individuals based on fear and ignorance, as well as trials that leave open the
question of whether justice has been done. Each volume begins by
setting the scene and providing a historical context to show how
society's mores influence the trial process and the verdict.

Each book goes on to present a detailed and lively account of the trial, including liberal use of primary source material such as direct testimony, lawyers' summations, and contemporary and modern commentary. In addition, sidebars throughout the text create a broader context by presenting illuminating details about important points of law, information on key personalities, and important distinctions related to civil, federal, and criminal procedures. Thus, all of the primary and secondary source material included in both the text and the sidebars demonstrates to readers the sources and methods historians use to derive information and conclusions about such events.

Lastly, each *Famous Trials* volume includes one or more of the following comprehensive tools that motivate readers to pursue further reading and research. A timeline allows readers to see the scope of the trial at a glance, annotated bibliographies provide both sources for further research and a thorough list of works consulted, a glossary helps students with unfamiliar words and concepts, and a comprehensive index permits quick scanning of the book as a whole.

The insight of Oliver Wendell Holmes Jr., distinguished Supreme Court justice, exemplifies the theme of the *Famous Trials* series. Taken from *The Common Law*, published in 1881, Holmes remarked: "The life of the law has not been logic, it has been experience." That "experience" consists mainly in how laws are applied in society and challenged in the courts, a process resulting in differing outcomes from one generation to the next. Thus, the *Famous Trials* series encourages readers to examine trials within a broader historical and social context.

Introduction

Deep Divisions over the Death Penalty

F*URMAN V. GEORGIA* REQUIRED the U.S. Supreme Court to decide one of the most controversial questions in American society: Is the taking of a human life by the state an acceptable punishment under the Constitution? Because capital punishment is a matter of life and death, it touches on people's core beliefs about right and wrong. As a result, the death penalty evokes strong opinions on both sides of the issue.

Demonstrators call for an end to the death penalty. Few issues arouse stronger feelings on both sides than capital punishment.

Most people who oppose the death penalty believe that all life is sacred and that it is immoral for the state to take the life of a condemned prisoner. Many of those who support capital punishment believe that criminal penalties must equal the crimes they punish and that it is immoral for the state to allow convicted killers to live when their victims are dead. Because the death penalty is mentioned in the scriptures of many religions, people on both sides of the issue often base their opinions on strongly held religious beliefs.

When *Furman v. Georgia* reached the U.S. Supreme Court in 1972, the American public was evenly divided over the issue of capital punishment. Public opinion polls showed that about 45 percent of Americans supported the death penalty and an equal number opposed it. Nine states already had outlawed the death penalty, and several others were contemplating doing so. At the same time, the legislatures in eight states had considered banning capital punishment but instead had voted to keep it.

Given the deep divisions over the death penalty, no one was surprised that the Supreme Court decided *Furman v. Georgia* by a one-vote margin, 5-4. The Court was not only split, but splintered. No more than four justices could agree on any of the major issues raised by the attorneys in the case. The fifth and deciding vote was cast on the narrowest possible legal grounds. In addition, each of the nine justices issued his own separate opinion—a rarity in the history of the Supreme Court.

Even after the Court handed down its decision, the public remained divided over capital punishment. Rather than settling the issue, *Furman v. Georgia* ignited further debate over it. Meanwhile legal scholars, legislators, and lower court judges struggled to understand the meaning and scope of the high court's decision. It would take several more years and numerous appeals before the Supreme Court would finally answer all of the questions raised by *Furman v. Georgia*.

For all its historic significance, *Furman v. Georgia* arose from the lowliest of human circumstances. Unlike the principals in other famous trials, William Henry Furman was not a leader, celebrity, or moral crusader. He did not intend to force his way into history, but through the back door of a stranger's house. His appearance in the annals of American law was a tragic and desperate mistake.

Chapter 1

Murder in Georgia

AROUND 2 A.M. in the morning of August 11, 1967, William Henry Furman approached a house in Savannah, Georgia, with the intention to break inside to steal something. The twenty-seven-year-old African-American burglar climbed the steps to the back porch, moved a washing machine away from the kitchen window, opened the window, reached inside the house, grasped the doorknob of the back door, turned it, and let himself in. A few yards away, the Caucasian man who lived in the house, William Micke, awoke.

A twenty-nine-year-old petty officer in the U.S. Coast Guard, William Micke was the father of five children ranging from one to fifteen years old. One of the Micke children, eleven-year-old Jimmie, was a chronic sleepwalker. When William Micke heard a noise coming from the kitchen in the middle of the night, he assumed that Jimmie was up again. "All right, Jimmie," William Micke called out, "let's get back to bed." [1] Micke got out of bed to help his son back to his room.

Micke's wife, Lanelle, remained in bed. She later said that she heard her husband's footsteps quicken as he approached the kitchen, then heard "a real loud sound and he screamed." [2] Frightened by the disturbance, Lanelle Micke gathered her children into her bedroom, shouted for the neighbors, and called the police. Fearful that an intruder might be in the house, Lanelle and the children remained in the bedroom until the police arrived. The investigating officer found William Micke lying in a pool of blood on the kitchen floor. He was dead.

A second police officer, Alphonso Hall, also responded to the call. As he approached the Micke residence, Hall saw a person

11

walk out of the woods nearby. Seeing the officer, the person fled. Because it had rained, Hall was able to follow the fugitive's footprints in the mud. The tracks led to a nearby house. Hall found William Furman hiding in the crawl space under the house.

Officer Hall later testified that he helped pull Furman out from under the house. Another officer searched Furman and found that he was carrying a gun. The officers placed Furman under arrest. Ballistics tests later identified Furman's gun as the weapon used in the Micke shooting. In addition, Furman's fingerprints matched those taken from the washing machine on the Mickes' back porch. Based on this evidence, the State of Georgia charged William Henry Furman with the murder of William Micke.

Furman had no money to pay for an attorney, so the court appointed one for him. B. Clarence Mayfield handled Furman's defense. Realizing that a plea of insanity might spare Furman's life, Mayfield asked the court to send Furman to the Georgia Central State Hospital at Milledgeville for a psychiatric exam. After observing Furman, the hospital staff reported that the accused killer suffered psychotic episodes. The hospital superintendent agreed with the diagnosis but concluded in a letter to the court that Furman was fit to stand trial. "He is not psychotic at present, knows right from wrong and is able to cooperate with his counsel in preparing his defense,"[3] the doctor wrote.

The Trial

William Henry Furman's trial in the Superior Court of Chatham County began at 10 A.M. on September 20, 1968. After a jury was selected and seated, the prosecution presented its case. The evidence showed that Furman broke into the Micke house and was standing in the kitchen when William Micke confronted him. Startled, Furman fled out the back door. Had he simply kept running, William Furman would have disappeared into the night and beyond the gaze of history. Instead, he fired a single shot toward the house as he fled. The bullet pierced the plywood door and struck William Micke in the chest.

Detective B. W. Smith testified that Furman waived his right to remain silent and to have an attorney present during questioning.

THE MIRANDA DECISION

Clarence Mayfield, Furman's attorney, claimed to the trial judge that his client had not been properly "mirandized" before he gave police statements incriminating himself in the murder of William Micke. The Miranda warning is now a standard feature of police procedure when a suspect is being questioned.

That warning is the product of a U.S. Supreme Court decision known as *Miranda v. Arizona*. In *Miranda v. Arizona* (1966), the Supreme Court ruled that "Prior to any questioning, the person must be warned that he has a right to remain silent, that any statement he does make may be used as evidence against him, and that he has a right to the presence of an attorney, either retained or appointed." The Court instituted this requirement to ensure that suspects are not intimidated by overzealous police or prosecutors into testifying against themselves, a guarantee of the Fifth Amendment to the Constitution. The requirement must be fulfilled whenever suspects are taken into custody or denied the ability to act freely by the authorities who wish to question them.

Ernesto Miranda had been picked out of a lineup in 1963 by a rape victim. Two hours later the police had a signed confession from Miranda. At his trial the police admitted that he had not been told what his rights were, but there was no evidence that he had been coerced by them.

The American Civil Liberties Union filed a friend of the court brief in the Miranda case, and one of its authors was Anthony Amsterdam, who would six years later argue before the Supreme Court in behalf of William Henry Furman.

The Supreme Court overturned the rape conviction of Ernesto Miranda (right) because the arresting police had neglected to inform him of his rights.

Smith said that Furman told the officers that he had shot Micke while engaged in burglary. According to Smith, Furman stated

> that he was in the kitchen; that the man came in the kitchen, saw him in there and attempted to grab him as he went out the door; said the man hit the door—instead of catching him, he hit the door, the door slammed between them, he turned around and fired one shot and ran.[4]

Furman later provided a different account of the shooting. Testifying in his own behalf, Furman stated that Micke's death was accidental:

> I admit going to these folks' home and they did caught me in there and I was coming back out, backing up and there was a wire down there on the floor. I was coming out back-wards and fell back and I didn't intend to kill nobody. I didn't know they was behind the door. The gun went off and I didn't know nothing about no murder until they arrested me, and when the gun went off I was down on the floor and I got up and ran. That's all to it.[5]

Instructions for the Jury

The attorneys completed the presentation of the evidence in midafternoon. After both sides had given their final arguments, Judge Dunbar Harrison gave instructions to the jury. Harrison started by providing the jurors with the definition of murder under Georgia law:

> Murder is the unlawful killing of a human being in the peace of the State, by a person of sound memory and dis-cretion, with malice aforethought, either express or implied.[6]

The judge explained that the use of a deadly weapon, such as a gun, implies malice. Harrison added that when an accidental or involuntary killing occurs during the commission of a separate crime, such as a burglary, that killing is to be considered murder. This kind of murder is known as "felony murder." Judge Harrison laid out the possible application of these laws to the specific offense of William Henry Furman:

TECHNICAL COLLEGE OF THE LOWCOUNTRY
LEARNING RESOURCES CENTER
POST OFFICE BOX 1288
BEAUFORT, SOUTH CAROLINA 29901-1288

If you believe beyond a reasonable doubt that the defendant broke and entered the dwelling of the deceased with
intent to commit a felony or a larceny and that after so
breaking and entering with such intent, the defendant
killed the deceased in the manner set forth in the indict-
ment, and if you find that such killing was the natural, reasonable and probable consequence of such breaking and
entering, then I instruct you that under such circumstances,
you would be authorized to convict the defendant of murder and this you would be authorized to do whether or not
the defendant intended to kill the deceased or not.[7]

Judge Harrison then gave the jury the instructions that would
have the greatest impact on the case of William Henry Furman.
The judge informed the jurors that they not only had to determine
the guilt or innocence of the defendant, but, if they found him
guilty, they also had to decide what his punishment would be.

*In 1968 when William
Furman's case went to trial,
Georgia law required juries to
choose between life in prison
or death by electrocution for
murder convictions.*

Georgia law provided two sentences for murder: death by electrocution or life in prison. Harrison stated that the jury could assign either punishment without having to provide any reason for its action. He added that the court would follow the jury's recommendation.

Guilty

At 3:35 P.M. the jury retired to deliberate. Within thirty-five minutes the jurors returned to the courtroom with a question. They asked the judge if they could return a verdict on the guilt or innocence of Furman and leave the decision about his punishment to the court. Judge Harrison stated that this was not possible. Georgia law required the jury to decide both the verdict and the punishment.

One hour later the jury returned to the courtroom with its verdict. The jurors found William Henry Furman guilty of murder. For punishment, the jury recommended a sentence of death. The judge ordered Furman to be executed by electrocution on November 8, 1969.

The Appeal to the Georgia Supreme Court

When Furman's one-day trial was over, B. Clarence Mayfield asked the court to grant his client a new trial on the grounds that Furman's constitutional rights had been violated. Judge Harrison refused. Mayfield then turned to the Supreme Court of Georgia, again arguing that Furman should receive a new trial because his constitutional rights had been violated. Mayfield claimed that the police officers who had interviewed Furman about the shooting failed to properly advise him of his rights before questioning him. This violated Furman's right against self-incrimination, which is guaranteed by the Fifth Amendment of the U.S. Constitution. Because Furman's statement that he had fired his gun toward the house was not obtained properly, Mayfield maintained, the judge should not have allowed the jury to hear it.

Mayfield also questioned whether Furman's Sixth Amendment right to be tried by an "impartial jury of the State" had been violated. Mayfield claimed in his appeal that one potential juror, Alvin W. Anchors, had been excluded from the jury because he expressed

Furman was sentenced to death by electrocution. His attorneys appealed the decision, claiming that the death penalty violates the Eighth Amendment's prohibition against "cruel and unusual punishments."

doubts about the use of the death penalty. Mayfield pointed out that the U.S. Supreme Court had held in *Witherspoon v. Illinois* (1968) that potential jurors could not be excluded from a jury simply because they had reservations about the death penalty. "A man who opposes the death penalty, no less than one who favors it, can make the discretionary judgment entrusted to him by the State and can thus obey the oath he takes as a juror," stated the Court. If all such people were excluded from juries, the Court reasoned, the result would be not just "a jury capable of imposing the death penalty," but rather, "a jury uncommonly willing to condemn a man to die."[8] Such a "hanging jury" would not be representative of the community in which the trial takes place, the Court declared, and thus would violate the defendant's Sixth Amendment rights. The Court added that only a potential juror who expressed an absolute unwillingness to vote for the death penalty could be excluded from a jury. Mayfield argued that because Anchors had not expressed such views, his exclusion from the jury had violated Furman's rights.

Mayfield also claimed that the Georgia statutes authorizing the death penalty violated the Constitution's Eighth Amendment prohibition against "cruel and unusual punishments." Traditionally, the Eighth Amendment had been viewed as prohibiting torture, but Mayfield argued that death itself was cruel and unusual.

In his request for a new trial, Mayfield maintained that Georgia's practice of allowing the jury to select between a death penalty and a prison sentence without any guidelines from the court was a violation of the Fourteenth Amendment guarantee of "due process." Mayfield pointed out that Georgia trial judges were specifically forbidden to instruct jurors on how to decide whether or not the death penalty was appropriate. Jurors were free to recommend the death penalty for any reason they chose or for no reason at all. Giving the jury such wide discretion, Mayfield reasoned, ensured that death sentences were handed out arbitrarily. This policy denied William Furman his constitutional right to due process.

The Georgia Supreme Court Rules

On April 24, 1969, the Supreme Court of Georgia issued a two-page ruling on Furman's appeal that rejected all of Mayfield's arguments. The Court held that Furman's confession was obtained legally, adding that Furman's statement alone would have been enough to establish his guilt in the crime of murder:

> The admission in open court by the accused . . . that during the period in which he was involved in the commission of a criminal act at the home of the deceased, he accidentally tripped over a wire in leaving the premises causing the gun to go off, together with other facts and circumstances surrounding the death of the deceased by violent means, was sufficient to support the verdict of guilty of murder.[9]

Furman's Sixth Amendment rights had not been violated during the jury selection process, the Georgia Supreme Court held, because Alvin W. Anchors had indicated that his attitude toward the death penalty would affect his judgment as to guilt. This admission provided the prosecution with a proper reason to exclude Anchors from the jury. The high court also found that the death penalty was not cruel and unusual punishment under the Georgia Constitution. The Georgia Supreme Court did not respond to the due process argument because, although Mayfield had raised the argument in his motion for a new trial, he did not emphasize it in his brief to the Georgia Supreme Court.

Since the Georgia Supreme Court is Georgia's highest legal authority, Furman had exhausted the appeal process within his own state. The only remaining court that might hear his appeal was the U.S. Supreme Court. Because Mayfield had maintained that the arrest, trial, conviction, and sentence of William Henry Furman had violated the U.S. Constitution, Georgia Supreme Court Chief W. H. Duckworth concluded that the U.S. Supreme Court might take an interest in his case. Duckworth granted Furman a stay of

A LITTLE-NOTED DISTINCTION

Just twenty-two lines of type in a single column in the *New York Times* of June 3, 1967, reported the execution the previous night of Luis Jose Monge in a Colorado prison. Perhaps Monge's execution did not warrant front-page coverage, but America's newspaper of record did not let his death pass without notice. The article began, "Luis Jose Monge died here tonight in the Colorado State Penitentiary gas chamber with prayers on his lips and a black rosary on his wrist."

Luis Jose Monge's 1967 execution was the last in the United States for almost a decade.

Monge had murdered his pregnant wife and three of their ten children in 1963. The *Times* said that as he was being led to the gas chamber, "He appeared pale but steeled for the death he had been ready to face since his arrest." Monge was typical of a distinct kind of killer: He welcomed his own execution. He had called the police after committing his crime, pled guilty, and refused any appeal of his sentence.

The article noted that Monge was only the second man executed in the United States in 1967, a pace far behind the historical norm, although it failed to note that executions were coming to a halt throughout the country. In fact, Luis Jose Monge would be the last man executed in the United States for almost ten years, until well after the Supreme Court ruled in *Furman v. Georgia.*

execution for ninety days so that his attorney could petition the nation's highest court.

The Legal Defense Fund Joins the Appeal

B. Clarence Mayfield filed a petition for an appeal to the U.S. Supreme Court on behalf of William Henry Furman, but his was not the only signature on the document. Six other attorneys— Anthony G. Amsterdam, Michael Meltsner, Jack Greenberg, James M. Nabrit III, Jack Himmelstein, and Elizabeth B. DuBois—also signed the petition. These six attorneys belonged to an organization known as the National Association for the Advancement of Colored People (NAACP), a civil rights organization founded in 1909 by a group of black and white citizens committed to social justice.

A black student ignores protesters as she arrives at Little Rock's Central High School in Arkansas. Integration of the school was ordered by a Federal court following legal action by NAACP Legal Defense Fund attorneys.

JACK GREENBERG

When John F. Kennedy made Thurgood Marshall an appellate court judge in 1961, Marshall selected Jack Greenberg, a white man, to succeed him at the NAACP's Legal Defense Fund. Greenberg had joined the Fund in 1949 at the age of twenty-four and remained with it for thirty-five years. During that time he represented Martin Luther King Jr. in Birmingham and argued before the Supreme Court for sit-in demonstrators and others, including rape defendants. At his direction the Fund brought about the desegregation of the Universities of Alabama and Mississippi. It fought for the speedy enforcement of desegregation rulings and civil rights laws in the face of widespread resistance. And, of course, there was some form of LDF support for virtually every death penalty appeal from the mid-1960s on.

Jack Greenberg was a crusader for civil rights during his thirty-five years with the Legal Defense Fund.

For much of Greenberg's tenure at the LDF there were tensions with the NAACP itself. At times the Fund's staff wanted to remove the "NAACP" from its name, and at times the NAACP wanted it removed. In one instance Greenberg agreed to have an LDF attorney take over the case of a rape defendant who had been previously defended by an NAACP attorney. How did the LDF get the defendant a new trial? By arguing that his previous counsel was ineffective! The NAACP sued the LDF in 1979 to claim funds contributed to the LDF. After Greenberg left the LDF to join the Columbia Law School in 1984, the suit was dismissed.

To help fight for the social, economic, educational, and political equality for minorities, the NAACP formed the Legal Defense and Education Fund (also called the "LDF" or the "Fund"). According to Michael Meltsner, one of the attorneys who signed the Furman brief, the purpose of the LDF was to "pursue equality for blacks by bringing test cases in the courts challenging the laws and customs on which racial segregation rested."[10]

Led by Thurgood Marshall, who later became the first black justice of the U.S. Supreme Court, the LDF had scored numerous legal victories on behalf of African-Americans. In 1935 the LDF won the right of a black student named Donald Murray to attend the all-white University of Maryland Law School. In 1954 the LDF won its most famous court battle, *Brown v. Board of Education of Topeka, Kansas*. In this landmark case, the U.S. Supreme Court overturned laws that created segregated schools, stating, "We conclude that in the field of public education the doctrine of 'separate but equal' has no place." [11]

The LDF Targets the Death Penalty

After winning *Brown v. Board of Education*, the Fund focused its attention on the way in which blacks were treated in the courts, especially the frequency with which blacks were sentenced to death. At first the LDF focused on death sentences for rape. Jack Greenberg, the lawyer who replaced Marshall as head of the Fund in 1961, wrote:

> we began exploring ways to attack the death penalty for rape. . . . We launched the effort because about 90 percent of the 455 defendants executed for rape since 1930 were blacks convicted of raping white women. [12]

The LDF soon found that its main arguments against the death penalty applied to all criminals sentenced to death, not just rapists. For example, LDF lawyers often argued that the exclusion of potential jurors who opposed the death penalty created the kind of "hanging jury" that the Supreme Court had condemned in *Witherspoon v. Illinois* (1968). Jury selection applied not only to rape cases, of course, but also to any capital crime. The LDF also attacked the practice of not instructing the jury on how to choose between a death sentence and a prison sentence. This, too, applied to sentencing in all capital crimes, not just rape. Finally, the argument that the death penalty was inherently "cruel and unusual" clearly applied to all sentences of death.

Just as the legal arguments that the LDF made against the death penalty applied to all capital crimes, so, too, did they apply to all people convicted of those crimes. As a result, LDF attorneys began to wonder if they should represent all death row inmates,

Legal Defense Fund attorneys George Hays, Thurgood Marshall, and James Nabrit III (left to right) after winning Brown v. Board of Education, *which overturned laws allowing segregation in public schools.*

not just African-Americans. This abstract question became a real choice when the governor of Arkansas signed the death warrants of six prisoners at one time. Three of the six condemned prisoners were LDF clients. The other three were not. The attorneys for the Fund promptly obtained stays of executions for their black clients. After discussing their options, the LDF attorneys decided that they could not in good conscience allow the three white inmates to be executed. Anthony Amsterdam, a law professor who worked with LDF lawyers, explained:

> We could no more let men die that we had the power to save than we could have passed by a dying accident victim sprawled bloody and writhing on the road without stopping to render such aid as we could.[13]

Law professor Anthony Amsterdam (center) was one of six NAACP attorneys who signed Furman's petition for appeal to the U.S. Supreme Court.

The LDF contacted the white inmates' last known lawyers and helped them obtain stays for the three men. The LDF began to do the same thing in other states as well.

Controlling the Appeals

Although the attorneys for the LDF were mainly concerned with saving the lives of all condemned prisoners, they also had a strategic reason for joining the cases of white prisoners. The LDF attorneys believed that the U.S. Supreme Court might be ready to review the constitutionality of the death penalty itself. Whatever the Court decided would likely set a precedent that would not soon be overturned. The LDF lawyers wanted to be sure that the best possible case was made against capital punishment, and they worried that other attorneys might fail to build a successful case. In his memoir, *Crusaders in the Courts: How a Dedicated Band of Lawyers Fought for the Civil Rights Revolution*, Jack Greenberg wrote:

We knew that if we wanted to persuade the Supreme Court to make law, we needed to control every case possible that involved capital punishment issues, or some lawyer with ideas quite different from ours or who was perhaps not very competent might produce decisions that would tie our hands. So, very soon we got into the capital punishment business generally, in murder as well as rape cases, representing whites as well as blacks, dealing with nonracial issues as well as racial ones.[14]

The case of William Henry Furman was just one of many death penalty appeals that the LDF wanted to keep under its control. Accordingly, the LDF attorneys approached B. Clarence Mayfield about letting the LDF join the appeal of the Furman case. Lacking experience before the U.S. Supreme Court, Mayfield welcomed the assistance of the LDF lawyers. Together the seven attorneys filed the petition titled "William Henry Furman v. State of Georgia." They then waited to see what the high court would do.

Chapter 2

A Traditional Punishment

W HEN THE U.S. Supreme Court reviews a case, it does not concern itself with matters of fact determined at the trial. Only judges and juries can decide guilt or innocence based on evidence. The duty of the Supreme Court is to make sure that laws under which people are tried and procedures followed by the police and the courts are in harmony with the U.S. Constitution. If the laws and their enforcement are constitutional, then lower court verdicts will stand. If the high court finds that a law conflicts with the Constitution, however, the Court can declare the law to be void. Likewise, when the actions of law enforcement officials or courts run counter to the Constitution, the Supreme Court can overturn the results of the trials or sentences.

The justices of the Supreme Court normally try to set aside their own personal beliefs and base their decisions instead on the principles, policies, and judgments set forth in earlier Supreme Court decisions. For additional guidance, the justices sometimes look beyond American law to the British legal tradition that preceded it. In rare cases, members of the Court may look even further back, to medieval and even ancient law, to understand the roots of the case they are reviewing. The appeal of William Henry Furman required this kind of historical review.

An Ancient Punishment

The sentence of death is as old as civilization itself. The ancient Persians, Greeks, Romans, Egyptians, Jews, and other civilizations

26

used death as the punishment for certain crimes. One reason that death was a common punishment was that no other penalty guaranteed that offenders would not repeat their crimes. Ancient people could not rely on imprisonment to protect society, because early forms of incarceration were far from escape-proof.

Death also satisfied the basic notion that the penalty should be as severe as the crime it punishes. "If there is serious injury, you are to take life for life, eye for eye, tooth for tooth, hand for hand, foot for foot, burn for burn, wound for wound, bruise for bruise,"[15] state the commandments that the Jewish leader Moses gave to his people around 1250 B.C. Under the laws of Moses, the sentence for William Furman's crime was death. "Anyone who strikes a man and kills him shall surely be put to death,"[16] state the ancient scriptures.

Adopted by the Christians and spread through Europe by the Christianized Roman Empire and the Catholic Church, the laws of Moses formed the foundation of Western law. For example, Alfred the Great (849–899), the Christian king of Wessex, one of the Anglo-Saxon kingdoms of England, echoed Exodus 21:12–13 when he decreed: "Let the man who slayeth another wilfully perish by death." [17]

An illustration of a man being drawn and quartered for murder in sixteenth-century France. Since the beginning of civilization, the death penalty has been used to punish people for such crimes as murder and rape.

Throughout Europe, the death penalty was used to punish crimes against people such as murder, rape, and kidnapping. It also was employed to punish crimes against the state, such as treason. In keeping with the biblical commandments, people found guilty of practicing sorcery and witchcraft were also sentenced to death.

The Equity of Crimes and Punishments

During the Middle Ages, European common law began to require a greater equality between crimes and punishments. As a result, the death penalty stopped being used in several of the instances called for in the Bible. Crimes such as adultery, swearing, and the cursing of parents were no longer considered severe enough to warrant the penalty of death.

The equity between crimes and punishments became a central tenet of British law in 1215 when King John of England, under pressure from his barons, affixed his seal to the Magna Carta. This charter guaranteed due process of law to the citizens of England, stating, "No freeman shall be taken, imprisoned, . . . or in any other way destroyed . . . except by the lawful judgment of his peers, or by the law of the land." [18] It also provided that punishments must not be excessive:

> A freeman shall not be amerced [fined] for a slight offense, except in accordance with the degree of the offense; and for a grave offense he shall be amerced in accordance with the gravity of the offense. [19]

A Ban on Cruel and Unusual Punishments

The equity between crimes and punishments established in the Magna Carta was affirmed and extended by the English Bill of Rights. Adopted by Parliament early in 1689 and given Royal Assent by King William III and Queen Mary on December 16 of that year, the English Bill of Rights called for equity not only in fines but also in physical punishments. "Excessive bail ought not to be required, nor excessive fines imposed, nor cruel and unusual punishments inflicted," [20] declared the document.

When English colonists settled in North America, they brought their charters, rights, and laws with them. The prohibition

An English army general is hanged for treason in 1780. Hanging was the most common method of execution used by English colonists in eighteenth-century America.

against cruel and unusual punishments applied to the thirteen American colonies just as it did in England. The death penalty also was used in all thirteen colonies. The Massachusetts Bay Colony listed thirteen crimes punishable by death, including idolatry and witchcraft. Hanging was the usual method of execution, but other methods, such as crushing with heavy stones, also were used.

After declaring their independence from England in 1776, the American states drew up new constitutions that reflected their British heritage. Virginia's Constitution of 1776 included a provision against cruel and unusual punishment as did the constitutions

THE SUPREME COURT'S ROLE

While the highest law of the land, the Constitution, goes into detail about the duties of Congress and the executive branch, it only outlines those of the highest court. Article III, Section 1 states:

> The judicial Power of the United States, shall be vested in one Supreme Court, and in such inferior Courts as the Congress may from time to time ordain and establish. The Judges, both of the Supreme and inferior Courts, shall hold their Offices during good Behavior, and shall, at stated Times, receive for their services, a Compensation, which shall not be diminished during their Continuance in Office.

Section 2 of that article lists the cases that the Supreme Court has the power to decide: "all Cases . . . arising under this Constitution, the Laws of the United States, and Treaties made." The Court would have the power to hear original arguments in cases involving foreign dignitaries and cases between states. In all other cases it would consider appeals only. Section 2 also specifies that trials shall be by jury and in the state where the crime was committed. Section 3 limits the charge of treason.

Congress and the Court itself were left to fill in the rest of the details. Neither Congress nor the Constitution gave the Court the right to review federal laws. In 1803, in *Marbury v. Madison*, the Court claimed this right for itself and has enjoyed it ever since.

---

of seven other states. Even settlers of the Northwest Territory were protected from cruel and unusual punishments under the Articles of Confederation.

The Eighth Amendment

Once the Revolutionary War was over, the founders of the United States added a Bill of Rights to the federal Constitution. The first ten amendments to the U.S. Constitution mirrored the English Bill of Rights in many ways. Both documents guaranteed "freedom of speech," "redress of grievances," and due process under the law. The Eighth Amendment to the U.S. Constitution was taken word for word from the English Bill of Rights. It states, "Excessive bail shall not be required, nor excessive fines imposed, nor cruel and unusual punishments inflicted." [21]

When the Eighth Amendment was being debated by the First Federal Congress, some delegates felt that its wording was too vague. Representative William L. Smith of South Carolina objected to the words "nor cruel and unusual punishments" on the grounds that they were too indefinite. Representative Samuel Livermore of New Hampshire agreed. "The clause seems to express a great deal of humanity, on which account I have no objection to it; but as it seems to have no meaning in it, I do not think it necessary," Livermore said. "What is meant by the terms excessive bail? Who are to be the judges? What is understood by excessive fines? It lies with the court to determine." [22]

Livermore was especially concerned that the vague words of the Eighth Amendment could be used to abolish the death penalty and other punishments he thought were necessary. "It is sometimes necessary to hang a man, villains often deserve whipping, and perhaps having their ears cut off," said Livermore. "Are we in future to be prevented from inflicting these punishments because they are cruel?" Fearing this might be the case, Livermore argued against the adoption of the amendment. "If a more lenient mode of correcting vice and deterring others from the commission of it could be invented, it would be very prudent in the Legislature to adopt it; but until we have some security that this will be done, we ought not to be restrained from making necessary laws by any declaration of this kind." [23]

Despite Livermore's criticism, the wording of the Eighth Amendment was not changed. When Virginia became the eleventh state to ratify the Bill of Rights in 1791, the protection against cruel and unusual punishments became the law of the land.

As Livermore predicted, the precise meaning of the Eighth Amendment would be determined by the courts. Article III of the Constitution provided that "all Cases, in Law and Equity, arising under this Constitution"

While drafting the Bill of Rights in 1789, the founders hotly debated the wording of the Eighth Amendment.

would be decided by "one supreme Court." [24] In *Federalist No. 78*, Alexander Hamilton stated that it was the duty of the Supreme Court to declare laws that conflict with the Constitution "to be void." [25] John Marshall, the fourth chief justice of the Supreme Court, took Article III even further. "It is emphatically the province and duty of the judicial department to say what the law is," [26] Marshall wrote for the majority in *Marbury v. Madison* (1803). Ever since *Marbury*, the Supreme Court has been the final arbiter of the meaning of the Constitution.

An Early Test of Capital Punishment

The Supreme Court was not asked to interpret the meaning of the Eighth Amendment's guarantee against cruel and unusual punishment until nearly a century after it had been ratified. In *Wilkerson v. Utah* (1879), the petitioner was convicted of murder in the first degree and sentenced to death by a jury. The presiding judge described the method of execution to Wilkerson, stating that: "Between the hours of ten o'clock in the forenoon and three o'clock in the afternoon of the last-named day you be taken from your place of confinement to some place within this district, and that you there be publicly shot until you are dead." [27] Wilkerson's attorneys appealed the verdict, claiming that the sentence violated the Eighth Amendment. They argued that allowing the judge to select the method of execution was unconstitutional and that death by firing squad was cruel and unusual.

The Supreme Court disagreed. Writing for the majority, Justice Nathan Clifford pointed out that although "the laws of the Territory contain no other specific regulation as to the mode of executing" a sentence of death, the Utah Territory penal code clearly leaves that decision to the court. "Revised Penal Code. Sect. 10 provides that 'the several sections of this code . . . devolve a duty upon the court authorized to pass sentence to determine and impose the punishment prescribed,' " wrote Clifford. Accordingly, the high court held that there was "no legal ground for reversing the judgment." [28]

As for the matter of whether or not death by gunfire was cruel and unusual, the Court admitted that the wording of the Eighth Amendment was somewhat vague. "Difficulty would attend the

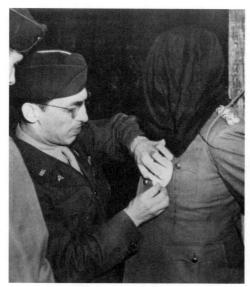

An American military doctor marks the heart of a Nazi war criminal before his execution by firing squad in 1945. In 1879 the U.S. Supreme Court ruled that death by gunfire did not constitute cruel or unusual punishment.

effort to define with exactness the extent of the constitutional provision which provides that cruel and unusual punishments shall not be inflicted," [29] wrote Justice Clifford. For guidance on the meaning of cruelty, the Court turned to the writings of the famous British jurist, Sir William Blackstone.

Blackstone described cases in which "terror, pain, or disgrace were sometimes superadded" to the sentence of death. "Cases mentioned by the author are, where the prisoner was drawn or dragged to the place of execution, in treason; or where he was embowelled alive, beheaded, and quartered, in high treason," Justice Clifford recounted. "Mention is also made of public dissection in murder, and burning alive in treason committed by a female." The Supreme Court found these "superadded" punishments to be unconstitutional. "It is safe to affirm that punishments of torture, such as those mentioned by the commentator referred to, and all others in the same line of unnecessary cruelty, are forbidden by that amendment to the Constitution," [30] stated Clifford.

After reviewing the many situations in which a firing squad was used to carry out a sentence of death, especially in the military, the high court concluded that death by gunfire was neither cruel nor unusual. "Cruel and unusual punishments are forbidden by the Constitution," wrote Clifford, "but the authorities referred to are quite sufficient to show that the punishment of shooting as a mode of executing the death penalty for the crime of murder in the first degree is not included in that category, within the meaning of the eighth amendment." [31]

An Unusual Punishment

A decade passed before the Court again faced a challenge to a punishment under the Eighth Amendment. By 1890, scientists and engineers had harnessed the power of electricity to create what was believed to be a more humane method of carrying out the death penalty: electrocution. In the case of *In re Kemmler* (1890), the attor-

An 1888 illustration depicts death by electrocution, which was touted as a more humane method of carrying out the death penalty.

EDISON V. WESTINGHOUSE

Late in the 1900s, Thomas Edison and George Westinghouse were competing to establish rival electrical systems. Edison favored direct current and Westinghouse alternating current. Alternating current had many advantages over direct current, but it had one major drawback: It was more lethal if handled carelessly.

Edison began a propaganda campaign against alternating current, stressing its danger and demonstrating its effect on animals. Edison suggested alternating current to New York state officials who were looking for a new, more humane way to execute prisoners. It was even suggested that thereafter one would speak of a criminal being "westinghoused," or being "condemned to the westinghouse." Westinghouse responded in letters to newspapers that asserted that alternating current was perfectly safe for household use and tried to stop the sale of any alternating current generators for use in executions. He was unsuccessful; New York made electrocution its method of execution in 1888.

The first electric chair execution did not go well. There was uncertainty about how much electricity to apply to the condemned. As a result, William Kemmler, whose case had been heard by the Supreme Court, revived after doctors had declared him dead. A second current was applied to him and killed him. The autopsy was postponed for hours so that the body could cool down.

---

ney for William Kemmler argued that the infliction of death by the application of electricity "is a cruel and unusual punishment, within the meaning of the constitution, and that it cannot, therefore, be lawfully inflicted." [32]

The Supreme Court upheld the lower court's finding that electrocution, though "certainly unusual," was not cruel "within the meaning of the constitution." Writing for a unanimous court, Chief Justice Melville W. Fuller noted that the State of New York had adopted the new method of execution for humane purposes. "The legislature . . . appointed a commission to investigate and report 'the most humane and practical method known to modern science of carrying into effect the sentence of death in capital cases,'" [33] wrote Fuller. No evidence was offered to show that electrocution caused anything but a painless death. After quoting from *Wilkerson v. Utah*, Justice Fuller offered a new definition of cruel punishment:

Punishments are cruel when they involve torture or a lingering death; but the punishment of death is not cruel within the meaning of that word as used in the constitution. It implies there something inhuman and barbarous, something more than the mere extinguishment of life.[34]

Excessive Punishments

Two years later, the Supreme Court again considered the issue of cruel and unusual punishments, although the case did not involve murder or the death penalty. The defendant in *O'Neil v. Vermont* (1892) was found guilty on 307 counts of selling liquor in violation of Vermont law. The court fined O'Neil $20 for each offense plus court costs for a total of $6,637.96—a huge sum of money at the time. In addition, the sentence provided that O'Neil, who was confined to prison, had to pay the fine by a certain date. If he did not pay the fine in time, he was to be imprisoned for 19,914 days (approximately 54 years) at hard labor. The Supreme Court upheld the sentence, but three justices—Stephen J. Field, John M. Harlan, and David J. Brewer—dissented. They found that the sentence violated the principle of equity between crimes and punishments. Justice Field wrote:

> That designation [cruel and unusual], it is true, is usually applied to punishments which inflict torture, such as the rack, the thumbscrew, the iron boot, the stretching of limbs and the like, which are attended with acute pain and suffering. . . . The inhibition is directed, not only against punishments of the character mentioned, but against all punishments which by their excessive length or severity are greatly disproportioned to the offences charged. The whole inhibition is against that which is excessive.[35]

Although the Court did not adopt the view of the dissenters in *O'Neil v. Vermont*, it followed their reasoning in two later cases. In *Howard v. Fleming* (1903), the Court rejected a claim that ten-year sentences for conspiracy to defraud were cruel and unusual. The Court found that the sentence of ten years was appropriate, but it

FRANCIS V. RESWEBER

In January 1947 the Supreme Court decided one of the most bizarre cases ever to come to it, *Francis v. Resweber*. Willie Francis, having been condemned to die in Louisiana's electric chair on May 3, 1946, was prepared for execution, put in the chair with witnesses present, and the switch was thrown. Soon it became apparent that the equipment had failed and Francis would not be executed. Francis was returned to his cell and a new execution date was set for six days later. Francis appealed and his case reached the Supreme Court.

Francis claimed a violation of the Fifth Amendment's prohibition of double jeopardy, or being put in danger of life or limb more than once for a single crime, and of the cruel and unusual prohibition of the Eighth Amendment. In essence, he felt that the psychological strain of preparing for execution could not be undergone twice without violating the cruel and unusual prohibition clause. The Court rejected both the double jeopardy claim and the cruel and unusual claim writing in the opinion known as State of La ex rel *Francis v. Resweber*, 329 U.S. 459 (1947):

Louisiana's first attempt to execute Willie Francis failed when the electric chair he was strapped to did not function properly.

> The cruelty against which the Constitution protects a convicted man is cruelty inherent in the method of punishment, not the necessary suffering involved in any method employed to extinguish life humanely. The fact that an unforeseeable accident prevented the prompt consummation of the sentence cannot, it seems to us, add an element of cruelty to a subsequent execution. There is no purpose to inflict unnecessary pain nor any unnecessary pain involved in the proposed execution. The situation of the unfortunate victim of this accident is just as though he had suffered the identical amount of mental anguish and physical pain in any other occurrence, such as, for example, a fire in the cell block. We cannot agree that the hardship imposed upon the petitioner rises to that level of hardship denounced as denial of due process because of cruelty.

The state later executed Willie Francis.

did so by using Justice Brewer's formula for weighing "the nature of the crime, the purpose of the law, and the length of the sentence imposed."[36]

The Court employed Justice Brewer's reasoning again when evaluating the sentence of Paul A. Weems in *Weems v. United States* (1910). Weems, an officer of the Bureau of the Coast Guard and Transportation of the U.S. government of the Philippine Islands, was convicted of falsifying a "public and official document." He was sentenced to fifteen years of "hard and painful labor" in prison. He also had to "carry a chain at the ankle, hanging from the wrists." Even after his release Weems was subject "to surveillance during life." Using Justice Brewer's logic, the Supreme Court struck down these penalties as excessive. The Court was especially concerned with the term "painful labor."[37] Justice Joseph McKenna wrote:

> What painful labor may mean we have no exact measure. It must be something more than hard labor. It may be hard labor pressed to the point of pain. Such penalties for such offenses amaze those who have formed their conception of the relation of a state to even its offending citizens from the practice of the American commonwealths, and believe that it is a precept of justice that punishment for crime should be graduated and proportioned to offense.[38]

The Court found that Weems' continued surveillance after release from prison also violated the principle of equity between punishments and crimes.

"New Conditions"

Although *Weems v. United States* did not involve the death penalty, it had a tremendous impact on later death penalty cases. Two of the justices, Edward D. White and Oliver Wendell Holmes Jr., disagreed with the majority that Weems's sentence violated the Eighth Amendment. They argued that the cruel and unusual clause was meant to prohibit "only those things that were objectionable at the time the Constitution was adopted." The majority rejected this "narrow and restrictive construction."[39] Writing for the majority, Justice McKenna announced that the Court could not be bound to past meanings of words included in the Constitution:

A 1920s portrait of the Supreme Court, including justices Joseph McKenna and Oliver Wendell Holmes (seated second and third from left).

Time works changes, brings into existence new conditions and purposes. Therefore a principle, to be vital, must be capable of wider application than the mischief which gave it birth. This is peculiarly true of constitutions. They are not ephemeral enactments, designed to meet passing occasions. . . . In the application of a constitution, therefore, our contemplation cannot be only of what has been, but of what may be.[40]

Justice McKenna emphasized that the Eighth Amendment must not be "fastened to . . . obsolete" ideas. The question the Court must answer is not whether a certain punishment was considered excessive at the moment that the Eighth Amendment was adopted in 1791, but whether it is excessive at the time the Court considers the case. Without such flexibility in interpreting the Eighth Amendment, the Court would be bound to uphold eighteenth century standards of criminal justice forever. Instead, Justice McKenna wrote, the Eighth Amendment "may acquire meaning as public opinion becomes enlightened by a humane justice."[41]

Evolving Standards

Four members of the Court expanded the doctrine of the Eighth Amendment's flexibility in *Trop v. Dulles* (1958). When Trop was convicted of wartime desertion, a military court stripped him of his U.S. citizenship. The Court found the punishment to be excessive. Writing for Justices Hugo L. Black, William O. Douglas, Charles E. Whittaker, and himself, Chief Justice Earl Warren declared that although the punishment given to Trop might not seem as bad as some of the punishments in force at the time the Constitution was written, it still could be excessive. The Eighth Amendment, Warren wrote, was not frozen in time but "must draw its meaning from the evolving standards of decency that mark the progress of a maturing society." [42]

While the Court did not decide if Trop's punishment was unconstitutional, Justice Warren's doctrine of evolving standards was cited by a majority of the Court four years later in *Robinson v.*

Chief Justice Earl Warren set forth the concept of "evolving standards of decency" with regard to the Eighth Amendment.

California (1962). In that case, the Court ruled that a sentence of ninety days in prison for violating a law against being "addicted to the use of narcotics" was cruel and unusual. Writing for the Court, Justice Potter Stewart affirmed the notion advanced in *Trop* that "the cruel and unusual punishment clause was not a static concept, but one that must be continually re-examined 'in the light of contemporary human knowledge.'"[43]

Opponents of the death penalty were greatly encouraged by the decisions in *Weems*, *Trop*, and *Robinson*. The doctrine of "evolving standards of decency"[44] meant that the Court was not bound by its previous decisions upholding the constitutionality of the death penalty. If attorneys for death row inmates such as William Furman could show that the death penalty was as barbaric and outmoded as whipping or the cutting off of a person's ears, then the high court might decide, as Livermore had predicted two centuries before, that society "might be prevented from inflicting these punishments because they are cruel."[45] All across the country, attorneys for condemned prisoners began to petition the Supreme Court to hear their appeals based on the argument that it was time to reexamine the death penalty.

The effort paid off. On June 28, 1971, the Supreme Court agreed to review several death penalty cases in order to answer the question "Does the imposition of the death penalty in this case constitute cruel and unusual punishment in violation of the Eighth and Fourteenth Amendments?"[46] From the dozens of death penalty appeals before it, the Court chose to hear four. It selected one case that involved a rape in which violence was used against the victim, *Jackson v. Georgia*, and one case in which a rape was accomplished by threats, *Branch v. Texas*. The Court also selected two murder cases: a brutal multiple murder, *Aikens v. California*, and one that involved the murder of a man who had gotten up in the middle of the night to investigate a noise in his kitchen, *Furman v. Georgia*.

Chapter 3

Death on Trial

BECAUSE THE SUPREME Court agreed to hear four different death penalty appeals on two separate grounds—violations of the Eighth and Fourteenth Amendments—the case that became known as *Furman v. Georgia* proved to be one of the most complex of the 1972 term. It also was one of the most important. The lives of 704 death row inmates hung in the balance.

Rather than relying on a single argument, the attorneys for the petitioners took a "shotgun" approach to the case, raising many different arguments at once. They reasoned that if one argument failed to convince a justice, another one might. These arguments broke into two main groups: those founded on the Eighth Amendment and those based on the Fourteenth Amendment.

The most obvious objection to the death penalty was that it violated the Eighth Amendment's prohibition against cruel and unusual punishments. Although the high court had held eighty years earlier that "the mere extinguishment of life" was not "cruel within the meaning of that word as used in the constitution," [47] more recent decisions had shown that cruelty was not a "static concept" but "one that must be continually re-examined 'in the light of contemporary human knowledge.' " [48]

A Lack of Support

To show that the death penalty violated "evolving standards of decency," [49] attorneys for the petitioners pointed out that the death penalty had been abolished in most Western countries where it previously had been used. England, France, Germany, the Netherlands, and Switzerland had all abolished the death penalty.

42

The death penalty abolition movement had gained strength in the United States as well. Many religious organizations, including the American Jewish Community, the Episcopal Church, the Presbyterian Church (U.S.A.), and the Lutheran Church in America, had gone on record as opposing the death penalty. By the time *Furman v. Georgia* reached the Supreme Court, ten states and two dependencies of the United States had abolished capital punishment. A 1967 poll conducted by the International Review on Public Opinion showed that just 42 percent of the American public supported the death penalty while 46 percent opposed it. Writing for the Supreme Court in *Witherspoon v. Illinois* (1968), Justice Potter Stewart characterized those favoring capital punishment as "a distinct and dwindling minority."[50]

Actor Marlon Brando (center) joins demonstrators against capital punishment outside the gates of San Quentin prison in 1960. The death penalty abolition movement gained considerable strength during the sixties.

To support the idea that capital punishment was outmoded and uncivilized, attorney Anthony Amsterdam, who represented both Furman and Aikens in their appeal to the Supreme Court, used a novel argument that he had first advanced before the United States Court of Appeals for the Fourth Circuit in a case known as *Boykin v. Alabama* (1969). Amsterdam argued that the American public tolerated the death penalty only because it was "sparsely and spottily"[51] applied. He pointed out that more than fifteen thousand homicides were committed each year in the United States, yet only about one hundred murderers were each year sentenced to death. Of these, only a handful were executed each year. Amsterdam claimed that if the death penalty were uniformly applied and carried out, the public would be outraged by the high level of state-sponsored bloodshed. He argued that under the Eighth Amendment courts must not allow "penalties so harsh that the public conscience would be appalled by their less arbitrary application."[52] If the public would not tolerate the widespread use of the death penalty, Amsterdam argued, then the Court must strike it down.

Judicial Interference

Attorneys representing Georgia, Texas, Florida, and California disputed the idea that the death penalty was obsolete and unpopular. They argued that many modern nations, including Canada and Australia, used the death penalty to punish serious crimes. More important, forty-one of the fifty states in the United States as well as the federal government had laws that called for capital punishment. California deputy attorney general Ronald George pointed out during oral arguments that eight other states had "experimented with abolition of the death penalty and rejected it." Noting that juries continued to return death sentences at a steady rate, George sarcastically suggested that the declining number of executions was due not to any change in the public attitude toward the death penalty but rather to "the evolving standards of our judiciary who have chosen to issue stays."[53]

Attorneys for the states also reminded the Court that former Chief Justice Warren, whose opinion in *Trop v. Dulles* had advanced

California deputy attorney general Ronald George disputed arguments that capital punishment had become obsolete and unpopular.

the concept of "evolving standards of decency," had acknowledged that the death penalty enjoyed popular support:

> Whatever the arguments may be against capital punishment, both on moral grounds and in terms of accomplishing the purposes of punishment—and they are forceful—the death penalty has been employed throughout our history, and, in a day when it is still widely accepted, it cannot be said to violate the constitutional concept of cruelty.[54]

The attorneys for Georgia, Texas, Florida, and California argued that even if the public was turning against the death penalty, it was up to Congress and the state legislatures, not the Supreme Court, to change public policy. The Constitution called for the Supreme Court to interpret the laws, not to make them. The Court had traditionally adhered closely to this principle; Justice Felix Frankfurter, in his concurring opinion in *Dennis v. United States* (1951), wrote: "Above all we must remember that this Court's power of judicial review is not 'an exercise of the powers of a super-legislature.'"[55]

The attorneys for the states pointed out that just one year before the Furman case, Justice Hugo L. Black had forcefully rejected the notion that the high court should make new law. Joining the Court's majority in upholding the death penalty in *McGautha v. California* (1971), Justice Black wrote, "Although some people have urged that this Court should amend the Constitution by interpretation to keep it abreast of modern ideas, I have never believed that lifetime judges in our system have any such legislative power."[56] He continued:

In McGautha v. California *(1971), Justice Hugo Black rejected the idea that the Supreme Court, rather than Congress and the state legislatures, should abolish the death penalty.*

HOW THE SUPREME COURT WORKS

For each case heard by the U.S. Supreme Court, there is a petition or appeal that introduces it to the Court, such as that of a condemned prisoner who hopes to have his sentence or conviction overturned, and the response of the opposing side, such as the state that prosecuted the case. Furman's petition was filed soon after the Georgia Supreme Court refused to order a new trial for him.

The Supreme Court reviews a very small fraction of the thousands of cases proposed to it each year. At least four justices must request that a case like *Furman* be heard before it is accepted. This is called "the rule of four." The cases it does select crowd the Court's nine-month term, and many of the decisions it makes as to which cases it will hear are made during its summer recess.

Once the Court has accepted a case, briefs are submitted and responded to by each side. These briefs carefully lay out the arguments propounded and respond to the other side's arguments. Soon after the Court is in session on the first Monday in October, oral arguments are heard. They last one hour for each case, with half given to each side. Justices often interrupt speakers to ask questions that they consider relevant. The justices' questions can severely limit the time available for a presentation in oral arguments, and unless an extension of the thirty-minute limit has been obtained in advance, a presenter may speak beyond the thirty-minute limit only to complete a sentence. After the oral arguments are heard the Court's members consider their opinions on the case at hand and a decision is written.

The Constitution grants this Court no power to reverse convictions because of our personal beliefs that state criminal procedures are "unfair," "arbitrary," "capricious," "unreasonable," or "shocking to our conscience.". . . Our responsibility is rather to determine whether petitioners have been denied rights expressly or impliedly guaranteed by the Federal Constitution as written.[57]

The Constitution "as Written"

Attorneys for the states argued that the Constitution "as written" did not forbid the death penalty. The attorneys pointed out that the Constitution refers to capital punishment three times without condemning it. For example, the Fifth Amendment states that a person charged with a capital crime must be indicted by a grand jury. It also states that no person shall be "put in jeopardy of life"[58] without due process of law. The Fourteenth Amendment, adopted more than seventy-five years after the Fifth and Eighth Amendments, also mentions the death penalty. Arguing for Georgia, Assistant Attorney General Dorothy Beasley stated that these references to capital punishment within the Constitution, and therefore the death penalty itself, could not be changed without the passage of a constitutional amendment.

The attorneys for the states also took a historical approach to defending the death penalty. They argued that since the death penalty was in use in all thirteen states at the time the Eighth Amendment was adopted, Congress and the states could not have intended for it to outlaw capital punishment. They again quoted Justice Hugo Black's opinion in *McGautha v. California:*

> The Eighth Amendment forbids "cruel and unusual punishments." In my view, these words cannot be read to outlaw capital punishment because that penalty was in common use and authorized by law here and in the countries from which our ancestors came at the time the Amendment was adopted. It is inconceivable to me that the framers intended to end capital punishment by the Amendment.[59]

The attorneys for the states argued that the purpose of the Eighth Amendment was not to abolish capital punishment, but only to ensure an equity between crimes and punishments.

The attorneys for the four condemned men also argued that the death penalty violated the Fourteenth Amendment's guarantee that "No State shall . . . deprive any person of life, liberty, or property, without due process of law; nor deny to any person within its jurisdiction the equal protection of the laws."[60] Like the case founded on the Eighth Amendment, the case based on the Fourteenth Amendment consisted of several different arguments.

Death for Rape

Representing one of the rapists who had been sentenced to death, Jack Greenberg argued that a sentence of death for the crime of rape raised a number of constitutional problems. For one thing, Greenberg stated, such a sentence violated the principle of equity between crimes and punishments. He echoed a point made by Justice Arthur J. Goldberg in his dissent from the Supreme Court's refusal to review the case of *Rudolph v. Alabama* in 1963, namely "whether the Eighth and Fourteenth Amendments permitted the death penalty for a rapist who had neither taken nor endangered human life." [61] Greenberg maintained that they did not. For support, he pointed to the fact that only a few states allowed the death penalty to be used to punish rape. On this basis, Greenberg argued that the death penalty for rape was "unusual."

Greenberg also believed that the death penalty was applied unfairly, which violated the equal protection clause of the Fourteenth Amendment. He noted that "90 percent of the 455 defendants executed for rape since 1930 were blacks convicted of raping white women." [62] Rapes of white women by white men, black women by

Nine black men accused of raping two white women in Alabama in 1931. Attorneys argued that blacks convicted of rape were far more likely than whites to receive the death penalty, and that it was therefore applied unfairly.

white men, and black women by black men, rarely resulted in a sentence of death. Greenberg pointed out that blacks were sometimes sentenced to death even when violence was not involved in a sexual assault. For example, in *Hamilton v. Alabama* (1961), a black man who broke into the home of a woman and exposed himself—without touching or threatening the victim—had been sentenced to death. The use of the death penalty against blacks who attacked white women caused legal scholar Michael Meltsner to conclude, "Capital punishment of rapists plainly reflected the exaggerated fear of a sexual contact between black men and white women in a segregated society." [63] Such discrimination was not allowed under the Fourteenth Amendment, Greenberg argued.

Racial Discrimination

The attorneys for the two murderers used a similar line of reasoning to attack the death penalty sentences of their clients. They argued that statistics showed that the death penalty was applied unequally

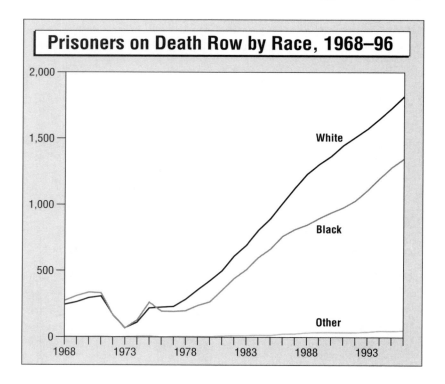

Prisoners on Death Row by Race, 1968–96

ANTHONY AMSTERDAM

Anthony Amsterdam, who argued for William Henry Furman before the Supreme Court, was the guiding hand for much of the Legal Defense Fund's work to repeal the death penalty. He worked tirelessly to prevent executions, but he also created the argument that became the battering ram in the battle to have the death penalty declared cruel and unusual.

Anthony Amsterdam was instrumental in the Legal Defense Fund's efforts to repeal the death penalty.

In December 1968 he began writing a friend of the court brief to be submitted in *Boykin v. Alabama* (1969). Boykin had pled guilty to five robberies that involved no killing and was sentenced to the death penalty. In that brief, Amsterdam formulated the definition of "cruel and unusual" that the *Furman* brief and oral argument embodied: that since capital punishment is used rarely and against only despised classes of people, largely racial minorities, the statute that authorizes it fails to express contemporary standards of decency.

The Supreme Court did not rule on this argument against capital punishment, but overturned Boykin's death penalty on the due process grounds that he had not been properly informed of the consequences of his pleading guilty. But Amsterdam's argument was planted. It would take time to have its effect. Indeed, it has. It was accepted by some of the Justices in *Furman*, and even today strands of the argument Amsterdam produced are still voiced against the death penalty.

across racial lines: Minorities were much more likely to receive the death penalty than whites were. Blacks were especially liable to receive the death penalty when the victim was white, as in the *Furman* case. "The figures are plain—the national prisoners' statistics—Georgia executes black people," [64] declared Anthony Amsterdam during oral arguments. Such discrimination, Amsterdam declared, violated the Fourteenth Amendment:

JUSTICE GOLDBERG'S DISSENT

Justice Arthur Goldberg's attention-drawing dissent in *Rudolph v. Alabama* (1963) was actually the remainder of a far larger work that he had prepared in the hope of turning his colleagues against capital punishment. Soon after President John F. Kennedy appointed him to the Court, Goldberg encountered troubling death penalty appeals. In some, racial discrimination seemed the only plausible explanation for the penalty's imposition, others showed evidence of a defendant's mental illness, and in others the defense counsel appeared incompetent.

In the summer of 1963, Goldberg had his law clerk at the Supreme Court, Alan Dershowitz, research precedents that would support abolition of the death penalty on the grounds that it violated the Eighth Amendment.

Justice Arthur Goldberg was a staunch opponent of capital punishment.

With Dershowitz he drafted a memorandum for his colleagues urging them to address the issue in six pending death penalty cases, even though the defendant's counsels had not raised the issue. He argued that not to address the issue was to approve of the death penalty. Short of abolition, Goldberg presented a number of reasons to limit the death penalty's application.

Goldberg's efforts failed. Not even Justices Brennan and Douglas, who had joined him in his *Rudolph* dissent, would agree to review the six cases he proposed to review. Two possible reasons for this rejection have been cited. First, the Court was already at the center of the civil rights storm preoccupying the nation—"Impeach[Chief Justice] Earl Warren" billboards were all along Southern highways—and, second, justices wanted to avoid any judicial approval of the death penalty so as to avoid damaging efforts in the legislatures or Congress to eliminate it.

What I am saying is that arbitrary, usually discriminatory, but unprovably discriminatory, infliction of punishment escapes all other constitutional controls—due process, equal protection—and escapes the public pressure to keep legislatures acting decently, unless there is something in the Constitution that forbids it.[65]

The attorneys for California, Georgia, and Texas agreed that the Fourteenth Amendment applied to the cases before the Court, but they disputed the idea that the petitioners' rights to due process and equal protection had been violated.

Arguing for Georgia, Assistant Attorney General Dorothy Beasley noted that the Fourteenth Amendment protects citizens from the arbitrary use of punishments, not from the punishments themselves. The Fourteenth Amendment even mentions the death penalty as one of the punishments that must be carried out fairly and justly. It was absurd, Beasley argued, for the petitioners to maintain that the Fourteenth Amendment guarantees the fair application of the death penalty and at the same time prevents the states from using the death penalty at all.

A Lack of Proof

The attorneys for Texas and Georgia claimed that the death penalty for rape was not applied discriminatorily. The reason that blacks received the death penalty more often than whites, they argued, was because more rapes were committed by blacks. They also produced studies showing that in Denver and Philadelphia, blacks committed twelve times as many rapes as whites did. Finally, they argued, death penalty statistics from the 1930s through the 1960s were too old to prove discrimination in the cases before the Court, especially considering changing racial attitudes and the due process guarantees that had been put in place in the previous decade.

The attorneys also disputed the suggestion that the death penalty was applied unfairly toward blacks and other minorities in cases of murder. Beasley included a chart in her brief that showed no discrimination against classes of people under death sentences. She told the court that even if discrimination were shown, that would not represent a case against the death penalty itself, but "would simply mean that in those cases where there was discrimination those sentences were invalid." [66]

Untrammeled Discretion

The attorneys for the petitioners launched one last plea on behalf of their clients, again relating to the due process clause of the Fourteenth Amendment. They argued that the juries meted out the death penalty without any guidance or standards. The *Furman* case was a classic example of arbitrary sentencing. Regarding the sentence, the judge only instructed the jury that they could reduce Furman's sentence to life in prison out of "mercy" for the killer. The jury did not have the benefit of a sentencing hearing, which might have helped them make their decision. Instead, the jury was required to decide both the guilt of the defendant and his sentence after only one hearing.

The problem with this approach, Anthony Amsterdam argued, was that the system did not distinguish between the kind of "regular garden variety burglary-murder"[67] that Furman committed and more heinous crimes committed by others. Under such a system, a person who killed several people could receive life in prison while someone who killed one person was sent to the electric chair. A person who tortured their victims before killing them might live out his life in prison, while someone like Furman, who shot his victim without really aiming his gun, received death. Such a system, Amsterdam argued, did not provide anything near "equal protection of the laws."

Attorneys for the states disagreed. They pointed to the Supreme Court's conclusion in *McGautha v. California* (1971) that creating specific guidelines for juries to decide which defendants would die and which would go to prison would have the effect of putting the jury into a straitjacket of standards. Rather than help defendants obtain due process under the law, such guidelines would limit the jury's ability to apply the evolving standards of society. Writing for the majority in *McGautha*, Justice John M. Harlan had stated:

> For a court to attempt to catalog the appropriate factors in this elusive area could inhibit rather than expand the scope of consideration, for no list of circumstances would ever be really complete. The infinite variety of cases and facets to

An attorney makes his closing statements to the jury in a murder trial. In 1971 the Supreme Court ruled against creating specific guidelines to help juries decide when to impose the death sentence.

each case would make general standards either meaningless "boiler-plate" or a statement of the obvious that no jury would need.[68]

It was better, the attorneys for the states maintained, to follow the Court's advice to leave "the power to pronounce life or death" to "the untrammeled discretion of the jury."[69] Since this is what the trial court in the case of *Furman v. Georgia* did, the states argued, its sentence should be allowed to stand.

Lives at Stake

In her closing arguments, Dorothy Beasley appealed to the Court to look to juries, which continued to return death sentences, and to the judiciary, which had never found the death penalty to be cruel and unusual, for a standard of what is acceptable in punishments. She added that the attorneys for the petitioners had failed to show that the death penalty was unconstitutional, even though the burden was on them to do so. Ronald George agreed. In his closing argument, George attacked Amsterdam's assertions as unfounded and urged the Court to consider the price that society might pay if death penalty laws were struck down:

> [Amsterdam] would have this Court become a superlegislature to enact his own personal views of what the evolving standards of our society should be. He has made no showing regarding the supposed lack of protection afforded by the death penalty, and if his argument were to prevail, indeed many persons might lose their lives innocently because of the removal of the protection of the death penalty.[70]

At the end of the oral arguments, the nine members of the Supreme Court withdrew to contemplate their decision.

Chapter 4

Split Decision

T HE SUPREME COURT normally takes several months to render its decisions. *Furman v. Georgia* was no exception. Five months passed from the time the Court heard oral arguments on January 17, 1972, until it announced its decision.

As in the case of Furman v. Georgia, *the Supreme Court generally renders its decisions several months after a case has been argued before the Court.*

57

The justices had many things to consider. First they had to decide if death was a cruel punishment in light of contemporary standards. If it was, then all death sentences would be struck down as unconstitutional. If death was not considered cruel, then the justices had to decide if it violated the equity between crimes and punishments. This was especially true in the cases of the two rapists who were sentenced to death. If the Court found the penalty to be reasonable, the justices then had to decide if it was being applied fairly. Was it being used to punish only the "outcasts" of society, as the attorneys for the petitioners had claimed, or was the disproportionate number of minorities on death row the result of social factors beyond the realm of the law? Finally, the Court had to decide if the method being used to sentence criminals to death met the Constitution's safeguards for due process and equal protection under the law.

A Decision Like No Other

The Court finally announced its ruling in *Furman v. Georgia* on June 29, 1972. Legal scholars were amazed at the complexity of the decision. Each of the nine justices had written his own separate opinion, tying a Supreme Court record. Together, the nine opinions ran more than two hundred pages, making *Furman v. Georgia* the longest Supreme Court decision ever issued. The Court split five to four on the issue of whether or not the death penalty was constitutional, but as *Time* magazine reported, the vote "was really closer than that."[71]

Human Dignity

Only two members of the Court, Justices William J. Brennan and Thurgood Marshall, found that death was cruel within the meaning of the Eighth Amendment. Although they agreed on this point, each justice arrived at his conclusion by different means.

Justice Brennan based his definition of the cruel and unusual punishments clause largely on the Court's finding in *Trop v. Dulles* that "The basic concept underlying the [Clause] is nothing less than the dignity of man."[72] Brennan continued:

JUSTICE THURGOOD MARSHALL

Thurgood Marshall was the first head of the NAACP's Legal Defense and Education Fund. Marshall began working with NAACP lawyers even before he finished Howard Law School in Washington, D.C. In 1935, in one of his first major civil rights cases, he and his mentor and professor at Howard, Charles Hamilton Houston, forced the integration of the law school at the University of Maryland. This was poetic justice: that law school had earlier rejected Marshall's application because of his race.

Justice Thurgood Marshall, the first black to serve on the U.S. Supreme Court.

Marshall's greatest legal victory was *Brown v. Board of Education*, which overturned the separate-but-equal educational system that *Plessy v. Ferguson* had established in 1896. Segregation in public education was made illegal by this victory of Marshall and a team of NAACP Legal Defense Fund attorneys.

President John F. Kennedy appointed Marshall to the U.S. Court of Appeals for the Second Circuit in 1961. In 1965, President Lyndon Johnson made him U.S. solicitor general and in 1967 he appointed him to the Supreme Court. He was the first black to ever serve on the Court, where he consistently opposed the death penalty. Marshall died in 1993. Today the law library at the University of Maryland is named after him.

At bottom, then, the Cruel and Unusual Punishments Clause prohibits the infliction of uncivilized and inhuman punishments. The State, even as it punishes, must treat its members with respect for their intrinsic worth as human beings. A punishment is "cruel and unusual," therefore, if it does not comport with human dignity.[73]

Under this definition, Brennan wrote, a punishment can be found to be unconstitutional if it is "so severe as to be degrading to the dignity of human beings." He reasoned that "pain, certainly, may be a factor in the judgment," but added that the Court found

In his opinion for Furman v. Georgia, *Justice William Brennan wrote that the death penalty is unusually severe and degrading to human dignity.*

in *Trop v. Dulles* that a punishment can be degrading even when "no physical mistreatment, no primitive torture" [74] is involved. Indeed, the punishment that the Court found to be cruel in *Trop v. Dulles* was the loss of citizenship, which "involves a denial by society of the individual's existence as a member of the human community." [75]

Another way to judge the constitutionality of a punishment, Brennan held, was to weigh how society viewed it. "Rejection by society, of course, is a strong indication that a severe punishment does not comport with human dignity," declared Brennan. The fact that many states called for the death penalty was not proof that society accepted it. What mattered, he reasoned, was whether society was willing to use the punishment. "The acceptability of a severe punishment is measured, not by its availability," Brennan wrote, "for it might become so offensive to society as never to be inflicted, but by its use." [76]

A "Unique Punishment"

Based on the principle that a punishment must preserve human dignity, Brennan devised a test to help define cruel and unusual punishment:

> It is a denial of human dignity for the State arbitrarily to subject a person to an unusually severe punishment that society has indicated it does not regard as acceptable, and that cannot be shown to serve any penal purpose more effectively than a significantly less drastic punishment. [77]

Brennan applied his test to death, which he called "a unique punishment in the United States." Noting that "no other punishment has been so continuously restricted," Brennan concluded that the "only explanation for the uniqueness of death is its extreme severity." [78] He continued:

> Death is today an unusually severe punishment, unusual in its pain, in its finality, and in its enormity. No other existing punishment is comparable to death in terms of physical and mental suffering. . . . In comparison to all other punishments today, then, the deliberate extinguishment of human life by the State is uniquely degrading to human dignity. [79]

Besides meeting the tests of being "unusually severe" and degrading to human dignity, the death penalty also met Brennan's test of being arbitrary. "When a country of over 200 million people inflicts an unusually severe punishment no more than 50 times a year, the inference is strong that the punishment is not being regularly and fairly applied," [80] Brennan declared.

Finally, Brennan found no evidence that the death penalty deters capital crimes any more than prison does, mainly because criminals do not think rationally about the consequences of their actions or, if they do, they do not believe they will get caught. "There is no reason to believe that as currently administered the punishment of death is necessary to deter the commission of capital crimes," Brennan concluded. As a result, Brennan found that the death penalty did not "serve any penal purpose more effectively than a significantly less drastic punishment." [81]

Finding the punishment of death to be "inconsistent with all four principles" guiding him, Brennan concluded, "Death is today a 'cruel and unusual' punishment." [82]

No Useful Purpose

Like Brennan, Justice Thurgood Marshall found, "There is no rational basis for concluding that capital punishment is not excessive. It therefore violates the Eighth Amendment." He arrived at this conclusion in a different way than Brennan did. "In order to assess whether or not death is an excessive or unnecessary penalty," Marshall wrote, "it is necessary to consider the reasons

Justice Marshall joined Justice Brennan in finding that the death penalty violates the Eighth Amendment's protection against cruel and unusual punishment.

why a legislature might select it as punishment for one or more offenses."[83] If a less severe penalty would achieve the same goals, Marshall reasoned, then the death penalty would be unnecessarily cruel, and, therefore, unconstitutional.

Marshall believed that capital punishment could conceivably serve six purposes: "retribution, deterrence, prevention of repetitive criminal acts, encouragement of guilty pleas and confessions, eugenics, and economy."[84]

Marshall dismissed retribution as a legitimate goal by pointing out that the "Eighth Amendment itself was adopted to prevent punishment from becoming synonymous with vengeance." He noted that in *Weems*, the high court ruled that "punishment for the sake of retribution was not permissible under the Eighth Amendment."[85]

Citing a United Nations study that found "no correlation between the existence of capital punishment and lower rates of capital crime," Marshall discounted deterrence as a legitimate purpose of capital punishment. Nor did Marshall believe that the death penalty was needed to prevent further crimes. Marshall cited more studies that showed "that murderers are extremely unlikely to commit other crimes either in prison or upon their release."[86]

Marshall found constitutional problems with the practice of using the fear of death to frighten defendants into accepting plea bargains that offered life in prison in exchange for a plea of guilty. "If the death penalty is used to encourage guilty pleas and thus to deter suspects from exercising their rights under the Sixth Amendment to jury trials, it is unconstitutional," Marshall declared. The death penalty could not be used to rid society of undesirable people, a practice known as eugenics. While admitting that "this Nation has never formally professed eugenic goals," Marshall nonetheless felt compelled to declare, "Any suggestions concerning the eugenic benefits of capital punishment are obviously meritless."[87]

The death penalty could not be upheld on the basis of economics, either, Marshall held. Whatever money the government might save by not feeding and housing a prisoner for a lifetime would be more than offset by the enormous cost of appeals. "When all is said and done," Marshall stated, "there can be no doubt that it costs more to execute a man than to keep him in prison for life." [88]

Having tested each of the reasons for keeping capital punishment, Marshall declared, "There is but one conclusion that can be drawn from all of this—i.e., the death penalty is an excessive and unnecessary punishment that violates the Eighth Amendment." By joining "the approximately 70 other jurisdictions in the world which celebrate their regard for civilization and humanity by shunning capital punishment," Marshall stated, the United States would "achieve 'a major milestone in the long road up from barbarism.' " [89]

Justices Brennan and Marshall were the only two members of the Court to hold that the death penalty is unconstitutional in all circumstances. The fact that the other seven justices did not join with Brennan and Marshall's opinions did not mean that the death penalty was constitutional, however. If three other justices found capital punishment to be unconstitutional, even if it was for other reasons, the death penalty would fall.

"The Law in Its Application"

Justice William O. Douglas also voted to strike down the death penalty. He did not agree with Brennan and Marshall that the death penalty was excessive and cruel. "It has been assumed in our decisions that punishment by death is not cruel, unless the manner of execution can be said to be inhuman and barbarous," Douglas wrote. He found problems not with the laws themselves, but with the way they were carried out. "What may be said of the validity of a law on the books and what may be done with the law in its application do, or may, lead to quite different conclusions," [90] he declared.

Douglas accepted Anthony Amsterdam's argument that death penalty sentencing was unfairly applied to minorities. "The death sentence is disproportionately imposed and carried out on the poor, the Negro, and the members of unpopular groups," [91] Douglas wrote. For this reason, Douglas reasoned, such sentences could not be squared with the Eighth Amendment:

> It would seem to be incontestable that the death penalty inflicted on one defendant is "unusual" if it discriminates

Justice William Douglas voted to strike down the death penalty based on the argument that it is unfairly applied to minorities and the poor.

against him by reason of his race, religion, wealth, social position, or class, or if it is imposed under a procedure that gives room for the play of such prejudices.[92]

An Unfair System

Douglas found that discrimination in death penalty sentencing was due not to unfair laws or bias on the part of juries. Rather, he wrote, discrimination arose from the relative wealth or poverty of the defendant. Douglas quoted Lewis E. Lawes, the warden of Sing Sing prison, who wrote:

THE WARREN COURT AND THE BURGER COURT

The campaign to induce the courts to eliminate the death penalty began during the Warren Court, or the period when Earl Warren was chief justice. *Furman v. Georgia* came early in the tenure of his successor, Warren Burger. Changes in the Court's personnel over these two courts changed the course of the death penalty's treatment.

Warren was a three-term Republican governor of California before President Dwight Eisenhower nominated him to the Court. The Warren Court (1953–1969) was characterized by an expansion of civil liberties and rights. Decisions such as *Miranda* and *Brown* made Earl Warren's name synonymous with liberalism for many Americans. Eisenhower is reported to have said that Warren's appointment was the worst mistake he made as president.

In May 1969, just a month before the resignation of Earl Warren, Abe Fortas, one of the most liberal justices on the Court, resigned. President Richard Nixon made known his intention to change the Court by appointing "strict constructionists," or justices who would abide by the Constitution more closely and not attempt to distort its meaning in order to implement their social goals. Nixon appointed Warren E. Burger to replace Chief Justice Warren and Harry Blackmun to replace Fortas. The changing of the Court continued with Nixon's next two nominations and under successive Republican presidents until near the end of the century. All four of President Nixon's appointees voted against the judgment in *Furman*, and these appointees voted to allow the death penalty in *Gregg* (1976). All of the Warren Court holdovers voted for the *Furman* judgment.

A 1962 photograph of the Warren Court (1953–1969), whose liberal opinions helped to advance the civil rights movement.

Juries do not intentionally favor the rich. The law is theo-
retically impartial, but the defendant with ample means is
able to have his case presented with every favorable aspect,
while the poor defendant often has a lawyer assigned by the
court. . . . The defendant of wealth and position never goes
to the electric chair or to the gallows.[93]

The intent of the law was not the only issue, Douglas maintained. Unintended results were just as important. To illustrate this
point, Douglas suggested that "a law that stated that anyone making more than $50,000 would be exempt from the death penalty"
would be unconstitutional. A law that said "that blacks, those who
never went beyond the fifth grade in school, those who made less
than $3,000 a year, or those who were unpopular or unstable should
be the only people executed" also would be unacceptable.
Although the death penalty laws as written did not contain such
blatant discrimination, they ended up having the same effect. "A
law which in the overall view reaches that result in practice has no
more sanctity than a law which in terms provides the same," [94]
Douglas declared. He continued:

Thus, these discretionary statutes are unconstitutional in
their operation. They are pregnant with discrimination and
discrimination is an ingredient not compatible with the idea
of equal protection of the laws that is implicit in the ban on
"cruel and unusual" punishments.[95]

An Ineffective Measure

Like Justice Douglas, Justice Byron White saw no problems with
the laws themselves, only with the way they were carried out. "I do
not at all intimate that the death penalty is unconstitutional per se
or that there is no system of capital punishment that would comport with the Eighth Amendment," White declared. In particular,
White did not believe that death was an excessive punishment.
"The penalty so imposed is not disproportionate to the crime and
those executed may deserve exactly what they received," he
wrote. The problem, White held, was that the Court was being

Justice Byron White concluded that because the death penalty was imposed infrequently, it served no useful purpose.

asked to uphold a penalty that in practice was becoming extinct. If a penalty is not being used, White reasoned, then it cannot serve any useful social goals. "Common sense and experience tell us that seldom-enforced laws become ineffective measures for controlling human conduct," [96] White wrote.

While admitting that he could not "prove" with "facts and figures" how infrequently the death penalty was being used, White concluded that "based on 10 years of almost daily exposure to the facts and circumstances of hundreds and hundreds of federal and state criminal cases involving crimes for which death is the authorized penalty" that "the death penalty is exacted with great infrequency even for the most atrocious crimes." Because the death penalty was so rarely imposed, White wrote, "the threat of execution" had ceased "to be of substantial service to criminal justice." [97] If the death penalty served no useful purpose, White reasoned, then its existence raised a constitutional problem. White wrote:

> The imposition and execution of the death penalty are obviously cruel in the dictionary sense. But the penalty has not been considered cruel and unusual punishment in the con-

stitutional sense because it was thought justified by the social ends it was deemed to serve. At the moment that it ceases realistically to further these purposes, however, the emerging question is whether its imposition in such circumstances

POTTER STEWART, SWING JUSTICE

Potter Stewart, who wrote the *Gregg* decision, came from an established family in Cincinnati. His father, James Garfield Stewart, was mayor of Cincinnati from 1938 to 1947. Potter Stewart attended prestigious Eastern schools, Hotchkiss and Yale, and returned from postgraduate studies at Cambridge University in England to enter Yale Law School in 1938. Stewart served in the navy during World War II.

Justice Potter Stewart was known as a "swing justice" while he served on the Supreme Court.

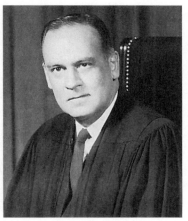

Stewart worked for Dwight Eisenhower during his campaign for the presidency in 1952. In 1954, Eisenhower appointed him to the U.S. Court of Appeals for the Sixth Circuit. In 1958 he became the last of five appointments that Eisenhower made to the Supreme Court. Stewart retired in 1981 and died in 1985.

Stewart was known as a "swing justice" because he moved between the liberal and conservative factions of the Court. He himself disliked the term, saying that justices should rule free of ideologies. In *Furman v. Georgia*, for example, he voted with the majority to overturn hundreds of death penalties on the grounds that the penalty was being unfairly administered. Later, in *Gregg* and other cases, he voted with the conservative majority to approve new death penalty laws that many states wrote after *Furman*. In *Griswold v. Connecticut* (1965), a decision that set the stage for the Court's legalizing of abortion, Stewart found Connecticut's law preventing couples from obtaining contraceptives "uncommonly silly," but he dissented from the majority because he found nothing unconstitutional about the law. The right to privacy cited by the majority, he wrote, is not to be found in the Constitution. In *Roe v. Wade*, the abortion ruling, he sided with the majority, saying that he "accepted" the principle of *Griswold* and the right to an abortion as a matter of privacy. Stewart wrote more than six hundred opinions in his time on the Supreme Court.

would violate the Eighth Amendment. It is my view that it would, for its imposition would then be the pointless and needless extinction of life with only marginal contributions to any discernible social or public purposes. A penalty with such negligible returns to the State would be patently excessive and cruel and unusual punishment violative of the Eighth Amendment.[98]

Like Justice Douglas, Justice White found that the constitutionality of a law depended not only on its theoretical intent but also on its practical use. "Legislative 'policy' is . . . defined not by what is legislatively authorized but by what juries and judges do in exercising the discretion so regularly conferred upon them," [99] White wrote. On this basis, White found death penalty laws to be unconstitutional.

Explicit Language of the Constitution

While Justices Brennan, Marshall, Douglas, and White found reasons that the death penalty was unconstitutional, four other justices argued just as forcefully that it was not. Justices Harry A. Blackmun, Lewis F. Powell Jr., and William H. Rehnquist joined Chief Justice Warren Burger in holding that the death penalty did not violate the Eighth and Fourteenth Amendments. "The explicit language of the Constitution affirmatively acknowledges the legal power to impose capital punishment," wrote Chief Justice Burger. "In the 181 years since the enactment of the Eighth Amendment, not a single decision of this Court has cast the slightest shadow of a doubt on the constitutionality of capital punishment." [100]

In his separate opinion, Justice Powell agreed that "cruel and unusual punishments" and "due process of law" are not "static concepts whose meaning and scope were sealed at the time of their writing." While agreeing that the Court was free to enlarge the meaning of phrases such as "cruel and unusual punishment" in light of "specific circumstances, many of which were not contemplated by their authors," the Court was not free to change their meaning completely. "While flexibility in the application of these broad concepts

Chief Justice Warren Burger stated that the Supreme Court does not have the constitutional authority to modify laws according to society's changing values.

is one of the hallmarks of our system of government, the Court is not free to read into the Constitution a meaning that is plainly at variance with its language," Powell wrote. "Both the language of the Fifth and Fourteenth Amendments and the history of the Eighth Amendment confirm beyond doubt that the death penalty was considered to be a constitutionally permissible punishment." [101]

Reliable Evidence of Support

Blackmun, Burger, Powell, and Rehnquist did not accept the argument that the public felt that capital punishment was barbaric and appalling. "There are no obvious indications that capital punishment offends the conscience of society to such a degree that our traditional deference to the legislative judgment must be abandoned," Chief Justice Burger wrote. "It is not a punishment . . . so roundly condemned that only a few aberrant legislatures have retained it on the statute books. Capital punishment is authorized by statute in 40 States, the District of Columbia, and in the federal courts for the commission of certain crimes." Burger pointed out that four times in the prior eleven years the U.S. Congress had passed laws calling for the death penalty for crimes such as the assassination of the president, the assassination of the vice president, and the assassination of members of Congress. For Burger, the willingness of Congress to impose the death penalty proved that it is still a socially acceptable punishment. "In looking for reliable indicia of contemporary attitude, none more trustworthy has been advanced," [102] Burger wrote.

Burger agreed with the argument that what is considered cruel and unusual will change over time, but he strongly objected to the notion that the Supreme Court should prohibit an existing punishment because society's values had changed. In Burger's view, it is the duty of the legislatures—not the Supreme Court—to modify the laws according to changing values. "In a democracy the legislative judgment is presumed to embody the basic standards of decency prevailing in the society," [103] Burger wrote. He pointed out that cruel and unusual punishments such as branding and ear cropping were eliminated by legislation, not by court decrees.

"A Tragic Byproduct"

Blackmun, Burger, Powell, and Rehnquist also rejected Justice Douglas's contention that discrimination in the application of the death penalty meant that it was unconstitutional. Justice Powell, who was joined in his opinion by Justices Blackmun, Burger, and Rehnquist, agreed that the death penalty "falls more heavily on the relatively impoverished and underprivileged elements of society." This fact did not disqualify the death penalty as a constitutionally acceptable punishment, however. "The 'have-nots' in every society always have been subject to greater pressure to commit crimes and to fewer constraints than their more affluent fellow citizens," wrote Powell. "This is, indeed, a tragic byproduct of social and economic deprivation, but it is not an argument of constitutional proportions under the Eighth or Fourteenth Amendment." [104]

In addition, Justice Powell was unable to see why the discrimination test should be applied to the death penalty but not to lesser punishments. "The Due Process Clause admits of no distinction between the deprivation of 'life' and the deprivation of 'liberty,' " observed Powell. Taken to its logical conclusion, Powell reasoned, the discrimination argument could be applied to all punishments. "If discriminatory impact renders capital punishment cruel and unusual, it likewise renders invalid most of the prescribed penalties for crimes of violence," Powell wrote. Such a judicial policy would have disastrous consequences, Powell suggested. "[No] society [could] have a viable system of criminal justice if sanctions were abolished or ameliorated because most of those who commit crimes happen to be underprivileged," [105] Powell concluded.

Justice Lewis Powell agreed that the death penalty is imposed more frequently on the "impoverished and underprivileged" of society, but rejected the notion that this fact rendered it a constitutionally invalid punishment.

Humanitarian Juries

Blackmun, Burger, Powell, and Rehnquist disputed Justice White's contention that the failure of juries to impose the death penalty weakened it as a punishment. Chief Justice Burger saw this line of reasoning as an attack on the jury system itself. He wrote:

> It is argued that in those capital cases where juries have rec-
> ommended mercy, they have given expression to civilized
> values and effectively renounced the legislative authoriza-
> tion for capital punishment. At the same time it is argued
> that where juries have made the awesome decision to send
> men to their deaths, they have acted arbitrarily and without
> sensitivity to prevailing standards of decency. This expla-
> nation for the infrequency of imposition of capital punish-
> ment is unsupported by known facts, and is inconsistent in
> principle with everything this Court has ever said about the
> functioning of juries in capital cases.[106]

A Narrow Decision

With four justices supporting the death penalty and four lined up against it, it was up to Justice Potter Stewart to decide if capital punishment would survive. Justice Stewart began his opinion by stating that he felt bound to confine his decision to the narrowest possible legal grounds. In doing so, Stewart followed the rules of judicial review laid out in *Ashwander v. Tennessee Valley Authority* (1936). According to those rules, "The Court will not 'formulate a rule of constitutional law broader than is required by the precise facts to which it is to be applied.' " [107] On this basis, Stewart declined to rule on the broad issue of whether or not the death penalty was unconstitutional in all cases. The only reason Stewart could think of for undertaking such a broad review would be if the laws under consideration automatically gave the death penalty to everyone convicted of a particular crime. Since none of the statutes before the Court did so, Stewart saw no reason to go as far as Justices Brennan and Marshall had. Stewart admitted that the case against the death penalty advanced by Justices Brennan and Marshall was "a strong one," but added, "I find it unnecessary to reach the ultimate question they would decide." [108]

*Although he joined the majority in deciding to overturn Furman's death sentence,
Justice Stewart declined to rule that the death penalty is unconstitutional in all
cases.*

Retribution

Stewart did choose to go on record regarding the topic of retribution, however. Several justices held that retribution was not a
proper goal of criminal punishment, but Stewart disagreed. "The
instinct for retribution is part of the nature of man, and channeling
that instinct in the administration of criminal justice serves an
important purpose in promoting the stability of a society governed
by law," Stewart wrote. "When people begin to believe that orga-
nized society is unwilling or unable to impose upon criminal
offenders the punishment they 'deserve,' then there are sown the
seeds of anarchy—of self-help, vigilante justice, and lynch law." [109]

The only issue before the Court, Stewart wrote, was the constitutionality of "a legal system" that produced the sentences of
death. Stewart saw some merit in the argument that the death
penalty was applied on "the constitutionally impermissible basis of
race," but he was not completely convinced that such was the case.

"Racial discrimination has not been proved, and I put it to one side,"[110] he wrote.

"Struck by Lightning"

Like Justice White, Stewart was disturbed by the reluctance of juries to impose the death penalty. "Of all the people convicted of rapes and murders in 1967 and 1968, many just as reprehensible as these, the petitioners are among a capriciously selected random handful upon whom the sentence of death has in fact been imposed," Stewart observed. Stewart could find no discernible reason why the death penalty was applied in some cases and not in others. "These death sentences are cruel and unusual in the same way that being struck by lightning is cruel and unusual," Stewart concluded. Without a rational basis for its application, the death penalty could not stand. "The Eighth and Fourteenth Amendments cannot tolerate the infliction of a sentence of death under legal systems that permit this unique penalty to be so wantonly and so freakishly imposed,"[111] Stewart wrote.

Justice Stewart joined with Justices Brennan, Marshall, Douglas, and White in voting five to four to reverse sentences of the petitioners. "The Court holds that the imposition and carrying out of the death penalty in these cases constitute cruel and unusual punishment in violation of the Eighth and Fourteenth Amendments,"[112] stated the majority.

The death penalty was dead, and the 706 men and women awaiting execution would live.

Chapter 5

After *Furman*

T HE SUPREME COURT'S decision in *Furman v. Georgia* left judges, legislators, attorneys, and legal scholars somewhat confused. On one hand the Court's ruling invalidated the sentence of everyone convicted of a capital crime under the laws in force at that time. On the other hand the Court did not say that a sentence of death would be unconstitutional at all times and in all circumstances.

A convicted killer on death row talks to a guard after learning of the Supreme Court decision in Furman v. Georgia. *He and hundreds of other inmates across the country had their death sentences commuted to prison terms.*

The decision handed down by majority emphasized that the "imposition and carrying out"[113] of the death penalty raised constitutional problems, but the penalty itself did not. The Court did not spell out what sentencing processes would be constitutionally acceptable.

After issuing its ruling, the Supreme Court remanded, or returned, the cases of the four petitioners to their respective states for further proceedings. On November 16, 1972, the Supreme Court of Georgia issued the following order to the Georgia courts that had sentenced thirteen defendants, including William Henry Furman, to death:

> The presiding judge in the trial court shall enter a judgment sentencing the defendant to be imprisoned for the balance of his life, this being the only lawful sentence which may be entered upon the conviction and finding of the jury that the defendant should receive the maximum sentence permitted by law.[114]

Hundreds of condemned prisoners across the country also had their death sentences commuted to prison terms. A few others received new trials.

Abhorrence for the Death Penalty

Those who opposed the death penalty were pleased by the Supreme Court's decision. They rejoiced that the lives of more than seven hundred condemned prisoners had been saved. They also took comfort in the fact that two members of the Supreme Court had condemned the death penalty outright. In addition, three other members of the Court—including two of the dissenting justices, Blackmun and Burger—expressed disgust at the taking of human life by the state. Justice Blackmun was particularly forceful in his condemnation of capital punishment, writing:

> I yield to no one in the depth of my distaste, antipathy, and, indeed, abhorrence, for the death penalty, with all its aspects of physical distress and fear and of moral judgment exercised by finite minds. That distaste is buttressed by a belief that capital punishment serves no useful purpose that can be

Justice Harry Blackmun expressed his abhorrence of the death penalty, but reluctantly voted to uphold it because he saw nothing in the Constitution that gave the Court justification to abolish it.

demonstrated. For me, it violates childhood's training and life's experiences, and is not compatible with the philosophical convictions I have been able to develop. It is antagonistic to any sense of "reverence for life." Were I a legislator, I would vote against the death penalty for the policy reasons argued by counsel for the respective petitioners and expressed and adopted in the several opinions filed by the Justices who vote to reverse these judgments.[115]

Blackmun voted to uphold the death penalty because he saw nothing in the Constitution that prevented Congress and the states

REACTIONS TO THE RULING

The *New York Times* of June 30, 1972, reported a wide variety of reactions to the *Furman* decision. Lucius Jackson, the rape defendant in *Jackson v. Georgia*, said, "I've been thinking of death for a long time. Now I can think about life."

In Nashville, Earnest Lee Herron, on death row for murder, said the ruling would mostly help "the poor and the black man": "The death penalty wasn't made for the rich man; it was made for the poor, the blacks and the ignorant."

Amid predictions that life-without-parole sentences would become commonplace as a result of the decision, Governor Jimmy Carter of Georgia said, "This decision clears the way for us to re-examine all our laws in Georgia. I still don't think seven years is long enough for a man to serve in prison who has committed premeditated murder and is given a life sentence." Later, in 1972, Governor Carter signed a new state death penalty law.

Jack Greenberg, then head of the Legal Defense Fund, said, "I think that there will no longer be any more capital punishment in America."

Richard Nixon, president of the United States, said that he hoped the decision "does not go so far as to rule out capital punishment for kidnapping and hijacking."

Governor Ronald Reagan of California said that he foresaw reinstatement of the death penalty in California for "cold-blooded, premeditated, planned murder," if a referendum on the November ballot passed. It did.

from having it, but his impassioned remarks reinforced the belief among death penalty opponents that capital punishment had fallen out of public favor.

Hope for the Death Penalty

Supporters of the death penalty read the Court's decision very differently. They saw that a seven to two majority of the Court had rejected the argument that the death penalty could not be allowed under any circumstances. "Today the Court has not ruled that capital punishment is per se violative of the Eighth Amendment; nor has it ruled that the punishment is barred for any particular class or classes of crimes," wrote Chief Justice Burger. The problem, Burger wrote, was a "deteriorated system of sentencing." [116] The flawed system, the chief justice suggested, could be remedied with new laws:

It is clear that if state legislatures and the Congress wish to maintain the availability of capital punishment, significant statutory changes will have to be made. Since the two pivotal concurring opinions turn on the assumption that the punishment of death is now meted out in a random and unpredictable manner, legislative bodies may seek to bring their laws into compliance with the Court's ruling by providing standards for juries and judges to follow in determining the sentence in capital cases or by more narrowly defining the crimes for which the penalty is to be imposed.[117]

New Death Penalty Laws

Congress and many state legislatures seized on Burger's suggestion that new laws might be drafted that would prove acceptable to a majority of the Court. By 1975, thirty-five states had adopted new death penalty laws. Some states, such as North Carolina, responded

Governor Ronald Reagan signs into law legislation reinstating the death penalty in California in 1973. By 1975 thirty-five states had passed new death penalty laws.

to *Furman* by adopting mandatory death penalties for a limited category of crimes. Other states, such as Texas, continued the practice of assessing each individual defendant convicted of a capital offense, but added new standards to guide the sentencing decision. Some states, such as Georgia, created two-phase trials, adding a sentencing phase after guilt had been determined. No one knew for certain if any or all of these approaches would hold up to the scrutiny of the Supreme Court.

On March 31, 1976, the Supreme Court heard the appeals of three men who had been sentenced to death under laws passed after *Furman v. Georgia*. One case, *Woodson v. North Carolina* (1976), tested the new mandatory death penalty adopted by North Carolina. The other case, *Gregg v. Georgia* (1976), tested the two-phase trial system that Georgia had created in response to *Furman*.

Woodson v. North Carolina

James Tyrone Woodson and Luby Waxton were convicted of first-degree murder for participating in an armed robbery of a convenience store in which the cashier was shot and killed and a customer seriously wounded. The evidence presented at the trial showed that Waxton shot the clerk at point-blank range while Woodson waited in a car parked outside the store. Both men were found guilty on all charges. The new North Carolina law required the two men to be sentenced to death.

Waxton and Woodson appealed their case all the way to the Supreme Court. Anthony Amsterdam argued the case for the petitioners, just as he had for Furman. Amsterdam again challenged the constitutionality of the death penalty itself. Once again, the Court did not accept this argument. "The petitioners argue that the imposition of the death penalty under any circumstances is cruel and unusual punishment in violation of the Eighth and Fourteenth Amendments," wrote Justice Stewart. "We reject this argument." [118]

Mandatory Sentences

As in *Furman*, however, five of the justices voted to strike down the sentences on constitutional grounds. Justices Brennan and Marshall

KENNETH ALLEN MCDUFF

In his closing arguments before the U.S. Supreme Court in *Furman v. Georgia*, California deputy attorney general Ronald George warned that "many persons might lose their lives innocently because of the removal of the protection of the death penalty." These chilling words proved prophetic a few years later when convicted murderer Kenneth Allen McDuff killed again.

McDuff was awaiting execution in Texas for the 1966 murder of three teenagers when the Supreme Court agreed to hear *Furman v. Georgia*. McDuff had killed two boys, raped a girl, then broken the girl's neck with a broomstick. Because of the brutal nature of his crimes, McDuff was sentenced to die in the electric chair. When the Supreme Court voided all death penalty sentences in *Furman v. Georgia*, however, McDuff's sentence was commuted to life in prison.

A rapidly increasing prison population caused severe overcrowding in Texas prisons. To alleviate the overcrowding, prison officials granted early paroles to thousands of inmates, including McDuff. Many people were shocked and frightened by McDuff's parole. In his book *Bad Boy from Rosebud: The Murderous Life of Kenneth Allen McDuff*, author Gary Lavergne wrote that in McLennon County, "Detective Richard Stroup reported that his office had been getting calls from housewives afraid to leave their kids by themselves during broad daylight."

The parents' fears proved justified. After his release, McDuff abducted and murdered two young women, Melissa Ann Northrup and Colleen Reed. Police arrested McDuff for the crimes and a jury found him guilty of murder. For the second time, McDuff was sentenced to death. In the weeks before his scheduled execution, McDuff helped authorities find the body of another of his victims. In addition, he was suspected of having murdered several other women in the Waco, Texas, area. On November 17, 1998, the state of Texas executed McDuff by lethal injection.

Two-time convicted killer Kenneth Allen McDuff (center) is escorted by law-enforcement officials.

Outrage over McDuff's parole and subsequent murders fueled demands for prison reform in Texas. In the mid-1990s, Texas vastly expanded its prison system, almost doubling the inmate population. In addition, new parole guidelines, sometimes referred to as the "McDuff Rules," were enacted to control the parole process more strictly.

again held that the death penalty itself was cruel and unusual. Justices Stewart, Powell, and John Paul Stevens found that North Carolina had gone too far in trying to eliminate arbitrariness from the sentencing process. While mandatory death sentences ensured that juries would no longer be able to impose the death penalty in a "freakish" manner, they also took away the juries' ability to consider any other factors in the sentencing. "The belief no longer prevails that every offense in a like legal category calls for an identical punishment without regard to the past life and habits of a particular offender," [119] wrote Justice Stewart, quoting from the Court's decision in *Williams v. New York* (1949).

The problem with mandatory death sentences, Stewart explained, is that juries often prefer to acquit defendants who are found guilty rather than execute them. "At least since the Revolution, American jurors have, with some regularity, disregarded their oaths and refused to convict defendants where a death sentence was the automatic consequence of a guilty verdict," observed Justice Stewart. This practice, known as jury nullification, undermines the legal system. "The history of mandatory death penalty statutes in the United States . . . reveals that the practice of sentencing to death all persons convicted of a particular offense has been rejected as unduly harsh and unworkably rigid," [120] wrote Justice Stewart.

The Character of the Offender

According to *Woodson v. North Carolina*, the sentencing process in a death penalty case must take into account the "character and record of the individual offender and the circumstances of the particular offense as a constitutionally indispensable part of the process of inflicting the penalty of death." Only by taking such factors into consideration could a jury find that "death is the appropriate punishment in a specific case." [121] Since the North Carolina death penalty law did not allow for this process, the high court found it unconstitutional. Justice Stewart wrote:

> The North Carolina statute fails to provide a constitutionally tolerable response to Furman's rejection of unbridled jury discretion in the imposition of capital sentences. . . . In

Oscar Collazo received a mandatory death sentence for killing a guard during an assassination attempt against President Harry S. Truman. In 1976 the Supreme Court declared mandatory death sentences "unduly harsh and unworkably rigid."

view of the historic record, it may reasonably be assumed that many juries under mandatory statutes will continue to consider the grave consequences of a conviction in reaching a verdict. But the North Carolina statute provides no standards to guide the jury in determining which murderers shall live and which shall die.[122]

Gregg v. Georgia

On the same day the Supreme Court struck down the North Carolina law, it also handed down its ruling on Georgia's new law in *Gregg v. Georgia* (1976).

Troy Gregg had been convicted on two counts of armed robbery and two counts of murder. In the penalty phase of Gregg's trial, the judge instructed the jury that it could recommend either a death sentence or a life prison sentence on each count. The judge added that the jury was free to consider any mitigating or aggravating circumstances presented during the trial. Finally, the jury could not impose the death penalty unless it found that Gregg's crime met one of three criteria set out under the law: "(1) that the murder was committed while the offender was engaged in the commission of other capital felonies, viz., the armed robberies of the victims; (2) that he committed the murder for the purpose of receiving the victims' money and automobile; or (3) that the murder was 'outrageously and wantonly vile, horrible and inhuman' in that it 'involved the depravity of [the] mind of the defendant.' " [123] At the sentencing phase, the jury found that Gregg's crime met the first and second of the "aggravating circumstances." As a result, the jury returned a sentence of death.

Under the new law the Georgia Supreme Court automatically reviewed the case. The state Supreme Court justices weighed the evidence presented during the sentencing trial and compared the jury's decision to decisions in other cases to see if the penalty was "unusual or motivated by prejudice or passions of the moment." [124] The Georgia Supreme Court also had to find that the evidence supported the finding of an aggravating circumstance. After its review, the Court upheld the death sentences for murder.

Convicted killer Troy Gregg, whose death sentence was upheld by the U.S. Supreme Court in 1976.

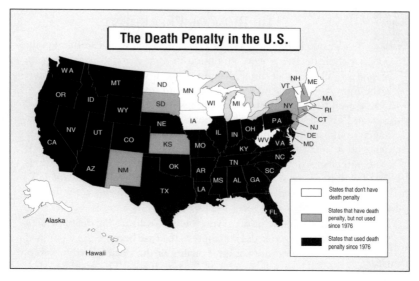

The U.S. Supreme Court voted seven to two to affirm the Georgia Supreme Court's decision. Justice Potter Stewart, who had written the narrowest and therefore most binding opinion in *Furman v. Georgia*, joined with justices Powell and Stevens to write one opinion upholding the death penalty in *Gregg v. Georgia*. Chief Justice Burger and Justices White and Rehnquist wrote a second opinion, which Justice Blackmun concurred, that also supported the death penalty. Justices Brennan and Marshall dissented, again holding that the death penalty is unconstitutional in all cases.

Public Acceptance of the Death Penalty

Gregg's attorney had repeated the argument advanced in *Furman* that the death penalty violated current standards of decency. The high court disagreed. As evidence that the public was not appalled by the death penalty, Justices Stewart, Powell, and Stevens pointed to actions taken by various legislatures since the *Furman* decision:

> The legislatures of at least 35 States have enacted new statutes that provide for the death penalty for at least some crimes that result in the death of another person. And the

THE ROLE OF PRECEDENT

Justices on both sides of the *Furman* decision were careful to point out that their decisions were grounded in *stare decicis*, or adherence to precedent. The respect the high court shows toward its earlier decisions is the foundation of its authority. If the Court reversed itself from day to day or even from term to term, its rulings would lose their meaning and power. The public officials who enforce Supreme Court decisions certainly would feel less obligated to carry out the Court's wishes if they believed it might reverse itself in the foreseeable future. In addition, if the Court changed its collective mind on a regular basis, it would be inundated with petitions asking it to rule on the same issue over and over. To avoid this kind of legal chaos and ensure that its decisions are enforced, the Court generally follows its earlier decisions.

In *Furman v. Georgia*, the justices who voted to overturn the death penalty maintained that *stare decisis* did not apply to the case because the Court had never directly ruled on the constitutionality of the death penalty before. "There is no holding directly in point," wrote Justice Thurgood Marshall in his concurring opinion. "The fact . . . that the Court, or individual Justices, may have in the past expressed an opinion that the death penalty is constitutional is not now binding on us," Marshall continued. In addition, Marshall reasoned, earlier decisions regarding the Eighth Amendment suggested that the Court must be flexible in interpreting the words "cruel and unusual," measuring them against contemporary standards of decency. "The very nature of the Eighth Amendment would dictate that unless a very recent decision existed, *stare decisis* would bow to changing values, and the question of the constitutionality of capital punishment at a given moment in history would remain open," Marshall wrote.

Congress of the United States, in 1974, enacted a statute providing the death penalty for aircraft piracy that results in death. But all of the post-*Furman* statutes make clear that capital punishment itself has not been rejected by the elected representatives of the people.[125]

For a second indicator of the public's acceptance of the death penalty, Stewart pointed to the willingness of juries to return death sentences. In the few cases when juries opted not to give the death penalty, Stewart continued, they were not demonstrating a universal rejection of the death penalty, as Anthony Amsterdam had argued in *Furman*. Rather, they were reflecting the standards of a humane society.

The dissenting justices strongly disagreed with the idea that the Court had not ruled on the constitutionality of the death penalty before. "All of the arguments and factual contentions accepted in the concurring opinions today were considered and rejected by the Court one year ago," Chief Justice Burger wrote, referring to *McGautha v. California* (1971). "If *stare decisis* means anything, that decision should be regarded as a controlling pronouncement of law." He continued: "It may be thought appropriate to subordinate principles of *stare decisis* where the subject is as sensitive as capital punishment and the stakes are so high, but these external considerations were no less weighty last year. This pattern of decisionmaking will do little to inspire confidence in the stability of the law."

Justice Lewis Powell agreed. "Less measurable, but certainly of no less significance, is the shattering effect this collection of views has on the root principles of *stare decisis*," Powell wrote in his dissenting opinion. "Petitioners assert that the constitutional issue is an open one uncontrolled by prior decisions of this Court. . . . I do not believe that the case law can be so easily cast aside. The Court on numerous occasions has both assumed and asserted the constitutionality of capital punishment." For this reason, Powell concluded, the majority in *Furman v. Georgia* had parted from the Court's long tradition of following its own precedents: "*Stare decisis*, if it is a doctrine founded on principle, surely applies where there exists a long line of cases endorsing or necessarily assuming the validity of a particular matter of constitutional interpretation. . . . Those who now resolve to set those views aside indeed have a heavy burden."

Adequate Guidance

Stewart then turned to the concern that he and Justice White had voiced in *Furman* that the death penalty not be "freakishly" imposed. Stewart and White were impressed by the two-phase trial system adopted by Georgia. The sentencing trial, or phase, Stewart wrote, allowed the jury to be "apprised of the information relevant to the imposition of sentence and provided with standards to guide its use of the information." The sentencing hearing and other safeguards, such as the automatic review by the Georgia Supreme Court of decisions resulting in the death penalty, made it unlikely that the Court would "impose a sentence that fairly can be called capricious or arbitrary." [126] Stewart concluded:

In summary, the concerns expressed in *Furman* that the penalty of death not be imposed in an arbitrary or capricious manner can be met by a carefully drafted statute that ensures that the sentencing authority [the jury] is given adequate information and guidance.[127]

As a result, the Court concluded, Georgia's death penalty scheme —and others like it—satisfied the requirements of the Eighth and Fourteenth Amendments.

Mitigating Factors

Other death penalty cases followed. The Supreme Court found death penalty procedures in Florida and Texas to be constitutional and those in Louisiana to be unconstitutional. In 1978 the Supreme Court considered a case testing the capital punishment laws of Ohio. In *Lockett v. Ohio* (1978), a unanimous Court overturned the death sentence of the petitioner. In doing so, Chief Justice Burger admitted that the Court's standards had been somewhat confusing. He wrote:

> In the last decade, many of the States have been obliged to revise their death penalty statutes in response to the various opinions supporting the judgments in *Furman* and *Gregg* and its companion cases. The signals from this Court have not, however, always been easy to decipher. The States now deserve the clearest guidance that the Court can provide; we have an obligation to reconcile previously differing views in order to provide that guidance.[128]

Burger pointed out that "there is no perfect procedure for deciding in which cases governmental authority should be used to impose death." He emphasized, however, that no death penalty process would be held to be constitutional unless it allowed the "sentencer in all capital cases" to weigh mitigating factors such as "the defendant's character and record" and the "circumstances of the offense." The lack of such guarantees, Burger concluded, "creates the risk that the death penalty will be imposed in spite of factors which may call for a less severe penalty."[129]

Utah became the first state to execute a prisoner after Furman v. Georgia *when it executed Gary Gilmore in 1977.*

With this guidance from the Court, Congress and the states passed additional laws calling for the death penalty. In 1977, Utah became the first state to execute a prisoner after *Furman v. Georgia*. Other states soon followed Utah's lead. The death penalty was once again alive and well.

Epiloque

Unintended Results

OPPONENTS OF THE death penalty had hoped that *Furman v. Georgia* would abolish it forever. Instead, it strengthened the punishment the abolitionists had worked so hard to destroy.

By voiding all death penalty laws and commuting all death sentences to life in prison, *Furman v. Georgia* shocked and outraged supporters of capital punishment. Death penalty proponents reopened the public debate on capital punishment with vigor. To the surprise of many death penalty abolitionists, the public rallied to support the ultimate punishment. In a statewide referendum the voters of California overwhelmingly adopted a constitutional amendment authorizing capital punishment, negating a ruling by the California Supreme Court that the death penalty violated the state's constitution. State legislatures across the country moved quickly to reinstate the death penalty. Politicians who had opposed the death penalty, such as Jerry Brown, Walter Mondale, and Michael Dukakis, were viewed by many people as "soft on crime." Every president elected after the reinstatement of the death penalty—Ronald Reagan, George Bush, Bill Clinton, and George W. Bush—supported the death penalty. By the turn of the twenty-first century, the death penalty enjoyed more support than at any time in the previous fifty years.

Since capital punishment was affirmed as constitutional, death penalty proponents have tried to streamline the execution process without violating the due process principles set forth in *Furman*. For example, the Anti-Terrorism and Effective Death Penalty Act of 1996, a federal law, limits inmates' access to federal courts after

92

state courts have reviewed their trial. The Supreme Court also ruled in 1989 that inmates are not entitled to be represented by court-appointed lawyers after their first round of appeals has been exhausted.

New methods of execution have contributed to increased public acceptance of the death penalty. Lethal injection, which kills the condemned prisoner by introducing toxic levels of drugs into the body, has been adopted by many states. Because lethal injection renders the prisoner unconscious before it actually takes life, many people view the procedure as more humane than previous methods of execution.

This is not to say that *Furman* had no effect at all on how the death penalty is carried out. Procedural changes adopted by states have decreased the chances that a person will receive the death penalty because of racial discrimination or for no clear reason at all. In addition, those convicted of capital crimes now have a way to bring mitigating factors to the attention of judges and juries, which might help them avoid capital punishment.

Increased fairness in the administration of the death penalty does not satisfy those who believe the death penalty is immoral. Opponents of capital punishment continue to fight against the penalty they abhor. In recent years instead of focusing on the ethics of the death penalty, opponents concentrate on its finality. They maintain that DNA testing and other evidence has shown that several people convicted of capital crimes were actually innocent. They point out that if the death penalty is used to execute an

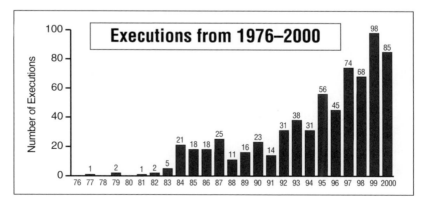

Executions from 1976–2000

As long as the death penalty remains in effect, opponents will continue their efforts to abolish it.

innocent person, the mistake cannot be corrected. In February 2000, Governor George Ryan of Illinois declared a moratorium (suspension) on executions in his state after a number of condemned prisoners were proven innocent.

Death penalty opponents also point out that execution takes away the possibility that someone who once killed might be rehabilitated in prison and become a responsible, productive member of society. As an example of a killer who was able to turn his life around, some point to the case of William Henry Furman, who was paroled in 1982. According to published reports, Furman has worked in construction and lived quietly in a boardinghouse. No further complaints have been filed against him.

Notes

Chapter 1: Murder in Georgia

1. Brief for Petitioner, *Furman v. Georgia*, quoted in Philip B. Kurland and Gerhard Casper, *Landmark Briefs and Arguments of the Supreme Court*, vol. 73. Arlington, VA: University Publications of America, Inc., 1975, p. 483.
2. Brief for Petitioner, *Furman v. Georgia*, quoted in Kurland and Casper, *Landmark Briefs*, p. 483.
3. Brief for Petitioner, *Furman v. Georgia*, quoted in Kurland and Casper, *Landmark Briefs*, p. 489.
4. Brief for Petitioner, *Furman v. Georgia*, quoted in Kurland and Casper, *Landmark Briefs*, p. 485.
5. Brief for Petitioner, *Furman v. Georgia*, quoted in Kurland and Casper, *Landmark Briefs*, p. 486.
6. Brief for Petitioner, *Furman v. Georgia*, quoted in Kurland and Casper, *Landmark Briefs*, p. 390.
7. Brief for Petitioner, *Furman v. Georgia*, quoted in Kurland and Casper, *Landmark Briefs*, p. 392.
8. *Witherspoon v. Illinois*, 391 U.S. 510.
9. Brief for Petitioner, *Furman v. Georgia*, quoted in Kurland and Casper, *Landmark Briefs*, p. 488.
10. Michael Meltsner, *Cruel and Unusual: The Supreme Court and Capital Punishment*. New York: William Morrow, 1973, p. 5.
11. *Brown v. Board of Education*, 347 U.S. 483.
12. Jack Greenberg, *Crusaders in the Courts: How a Dedicated Band of Lawyers Fought for the Civil Rights Revolution*. New York: BasicBooks, 1994, p. 440.
13. Quoted in Meltsner, *Cruel and Unusual*, p. 108.
14. Greenberg, *Crusaders in the Courts*, p. 443.

Chapter 2: A Traditional Punishment

15. New International Version, Exodus 21:23–25, www.bible.gospel com.net/bible?passage=EXOD+21&language=english&version=NIV&showfn=on.
16. New International Version, Exodus 21:12.

17. Laws of Alfred.
18. Magna Carta.
19. Magna Carta.
20. English Bill of Rights.
21. U.S. Constitution, Eighth Amendment.
22. Quoted in *Furman v. Georgia*, 408 U.S. 238.
23. Quoted in *Furman v. Georgia*, 408 U.S. 238.
24. U.S. Constitution, Article III.
25. *Federalist No. 78.*
26. *Marbury v. Madison*, 5 U.S. 137.
27. *Wilkerson v. Utah*, 99 U.S. 130.
28. *Wilkerson v. Utah*, 99 U.S. 130.
29. *Wilkerson v. Utah*, 99 U.S. 130.
30. *Wilkerson v. Utah*, 99 U.S. 130.
31. *Wilkerson v. Utah*, 99 U.S. 130.
32. *In re Kemmler*, 136 U.S. 436.
33. *In re Kemmler*, 136 U.S. 436.
34. *In re Kemmler*, 136 U.S. 436.
35. *O'Neil v. Vermont*, 144 U.S. 323.
36. *O'Neil v. Vermont*, 144 U.S. 323.
37. *Weems v. United States*, 217 U.S. 349.
38. *Weems v. United States*, 217 U.S. 349.
39. *Weems v. United States*, 217 U.S. 349.
40. *Weems v. United States*, 217 U.S. 349.
41. *Weems v. United States*, 217 U.S. 349.
42. *Trop v. Dulles*, 356 U.S. 86.
43. *Robinson v. California*, 370 U.S. 660.
44. *Trop v. Dulles*, 356 U.S. 86.
45. Quoted in *Furman v. Georgia*, 408 U.S. 238.
46. *Furman v. Georgia*, 408 U.S. 238.

Chapter 3: Death on Trial

47. *Wilkerson v. Utah*, 99 U.S. 130.
48. *Robinson v. California*, 370 U.S. 660.
49. *Trop v. Dulles*, 356 U.S. 86.
50. *Witherspoon v. Illinois*, 391 U.S. 510
51. Quoted in Meltsner, *Cruel and Unusual*, p. 182.

52. *Boykin v. Alabama*, 395 U.S. 238.
53. Quoted in Kurland and Casper, *Landmark Briefs*, p. 849.
54. *Trop v. Dulles*, 356 U.S. 86.
55. *McGautha v. California*, 502 U.S. 183.
56. *McGautha v. California*, 502 U.S. 183.
57. *McGautha v. California*, 502 U.S. 183.
58. U.S. Constitution, Fifth Amendment.
59. *McGautha v. California*, 502 U.S. 183.
60. U.S. Constitution, Fourteenth Amendment.
61. Greenberg, *Crusaders in the Courts*, p. 441.
62. Greenberg, *Crusaders in the Courts*, p. 440.
63. Meltsner, *Cruel and Unusual*, p. 76.
64. Quoted in Kurland and Casper, *Landmark Briefs*, p. 861.
65. Quoted in Kurland and Casper, *Landmark Briefs*, p. 873.
66. Quoted in Kurland and Casper, *Landmark Briefs*, p. 869.
67. Quoted in Kurland and Casper, *Landmark Briefs*, p. 872.
68. *McGautha v. California*, 502 U.S. 183.
69. *McGautha v. California*, 502 U.S. 183.
70. Quoted in Kurland and Casper, *Landmark Briefs*, p. 852.

Chapter 4: Split Decision

71. *Time*, July 10, 1972.
72. *Trop v. Dulles*, 356 U.S. 86.
73. *Furman v. Georgia*, 408 U.S. 238.
74. *Furman v. Georgia*, 408 U.S. 238.
75. *Trop v. Dulles*, 356 U.S. 86.
76. *Furman v. Georgia*, 408 U.S. 238.
77. *Furman v. Georgia*, 408 U.S. 238.
78. *Furman v. Georgia*, 408 U.S. 238.
79. *Furman v. Georgia*, 408 U.S. 238.
80. *Furman v. Georgia*, 408 U.S. 238.
81. *Furman v. Georgia*, 408 U.S. 238.
82. *Furman v. Georgia*, 408 U.S. 238.
83. *Furman v. Georgia*, 408 U.S. 238.
84. *Furman v. Georgia*, 408 U.S. 238.
85. *Furman v. Georgia*, 408 U.S. 238.
86. *Furman v. Georgia*, 408 U.S. 238.
87. *Furman v. Georgia*, 408 U.S. 238.

88. *Furman v. Georgia*, 408 U.S. 238.

89. *Furman v. Georgia*, 408 U.S. 238.

90. *Furman v. Georgia*, 408 U.S. 238.

91. *Furman v. Georgia*, 408 U.S. 238.

92. *Furman v. Georgia*, 408 U.S. 238.

93. *Furman v. Georgia*, 408 U.S. 238.

94. *Furman v. Georgia*, 408 U.S. 238.

95. *Furman v. Georgia*, 408 U.S. 238.

96. *Furman v. Georgia*, 408 U.S. 238.

97. *Furman v. Georgia*, 408 U.S. 238.

98. *Furman v. Georgia*, 408 U.S. 238.

99. *Furman v. Georgia*, 408 U.S. 238.

100. *Furman v. Georgia*, 408 U.S. 238.

101. *Furman v. Georgia*, 408 U.S. 238.

102. *Furman v. Georgia*, 408 U.S. 238.

103. *Furman v. Georgia*, 408 U.S. 238.

104. *Furman v. Georgia*, 408 U.S. 238.

105. *Furman v. Georgia*, 408 U.S. 238.

106. *Furman v. Georgia*, 408 U.S. 238.

107. *Ashwander v. Tennessee Valley Authority*, 297 U.S. 288.

108. *Furman v. Georgia*, 408 U.S. 238.

109. *Furman v. Georgia*, 408 U.S. 238.

110. *Furman v. Georgia*, 408 U.S. 238.

111. *Furman v. Georgia*, 408 U.S. 238.

112. *Furman v. Georgia*, 408 U.S. 238.

Chapter 5: After *Furman*

113. *Furman v. Georgia*, 408 U.S. 238.

114. 229 Ga. 731, 194 S.E.2d 410.

115. *Furman v. Georgia*, 408 U.S. 238.

116. *Furman v. Georgia*, 408 U.S. 238.

117. *Furman v. Georgia*, 408 U.S. 238.

118. *Woodson v. North Carolina*, 428 U.S. 280.

119. *Woodson v. North Carolina*, 428 U.S. 280.

120. *Woodson v. North Carolina*, 428 U.S. 280.

121. *Woodson v. North Carolina*, 428 U.S. 280.

122. *Woodson v. North Carolina*, 428 U.S. 280.

123. *Gregg v. Georgia*, 428 U.S. 153.

124. *Gregg v. Georgia*, 428 U.S. 153.
125. *Gregg v. Georgia*, 428 U.S. 153.
126. *Gregg v. Georgia*, 428 U.S. 153.
127. *Gregg v. Georgia*, 428 U.S. 153.
128. *Lockett v. Ohio*, 438 U.S. 586.
129. *Lockett v. Ohio*, 438 U.S. 586.

For Further Reading

Books

Joan Biskupic and Elder Witt, *The Supreme Court at Work*, 2nd ed. Washington, DC: Congressional Quarterly, 1997. Excellent brief history of the Supreme Court, its justices, and important cases.

Vincent Buranelli, *The Eighth Amendment.* Englewood Cliffs: Silver Burdett Press, 1991. Introduction by Warren E. Burger, chief justice for the *Furman* case. A fairly easy to read and short book on the amendment that forbids cruel and unusual punishment.

Jack Greenberg, *Crusaders in the Courts: How a Dedicated Band of Lawyers Fought for the Civil Rights Revolution.* New York: Basic-Books, 1994. A detailed account of all the NAACP Legal Defense Fund's efforts, including the school desegregation and death penalty campaigns.

Wendy Kaminer, *It's All the Rage: Crime and Culture.* Reading, MA: Addison-Wesley, 1995. An analysis of cultural factors related to the death penalty and of pro-and-con arguments. The author is a former public defender.

Michael Meltsner, *Cruel and Unusual: The Supreme Court and Capital Punishment.* New York: William Morrow, 1973. A brief history of the LDF's campaign (by one of its attorneys) against the death penalty through *Furman v. Georgia.*

Ernst van den Haag and John P. Conrad, *The Death Penalty: A Debate.* New York: Plenum Press, 1983. A debate between the abolitionist Conrad and van den Haag on most major issues related to the death penalty. Van den Haag's arguments in favor of the death penalty have been cited often over the years.

Internet Sources

John Gettings, "Worldwide Death Penalty Update: Here and Abroad," Infoplease.com, www.infoplease.com/spot/deathworld 1.html. Brief introduction to the subject with links to recent articles and statistics.

Websites

Findlaw.com. Invaluable resource, since most libraries do not have complete Supreme Court decisions. Offers virtually every Supreme Court decision, with every justice's opinion in its entirety with footnotes. Justices' references to other decisions are linked to those decisions. All Supreme Court decision quotations in this book are from this website.

Works Consulted

Books

Hugo Adam Bedau, ed., *The Death Penalty in America: Current Controversies*. New York: Oxford University Press, 1997. Contains a brief history of the death penalty in America, state-by-state statistics of every imaginable related sort, and essays pro and con on the death penalty. Bedau helped in the NAACP Legal Defense Fund's campaign against the death penalty and argues strongly against it.

Michael Davis and Hunter R. Clark, *Thurgood Marshall: Warrior at the Bar, Rebel on the Bench*. New York: Carol Publishing Group, 1992. An admiring biography of the first head of the NAACP's Legal Defense Fund and later Supreme Court justice.

Philip B. Kurland and Gerhard Casper, *Landmark Briefs and Arguments of the Supreme Court*. Vol. 73. Arlington, VA: University Publications of America, Inc., 1975. Contains the Supreme Court petitions, briefs, friend of the court briefs, and oral arguments for the states and defendants in *Furman v. Georgia*.

David M. O'Brien, *Constitutional Law and Politics: Civil Rights and Civil Liberties*. Vol. 2. New York: W. W. Norton, 1991. A vast constitutional law textbook that covers much in addition to the development of Eighth and Fourteenth Amendment death penalty law.

Periodicals

Martin Arnold, "Parole in Capital Offenses Less Likely, Officials Say," *New York Times*, June 30, 1972.

Tom Goldstein, "Inmates' Lawyers Report Many May Face Execution," *New York Times*, July 3, 1976.

Fred P. Graham, "700 Await Court's Verdict," *New York Times*, January 23, 1972.

Fred P. Graham, "Supreme Court, 5-4, Bars Death Penalty as It Is Imposed Under Present Statutes," *New York Times*, June 30, 1972.

Richard Halloran, "Death Penalties Argued in Court," *New York Times*, January 18, 1972.

Scott W. Howe, "The Failed Case for Eighth Amendment Regulation of the Capital Sentencing Trial," *University of Pennsylvania Law Review*, March 1998.

Paul L. Montgomery, "Penalty Limited by 37 Countries," *New York Times*, June 30, 1972.

New York Times, "The High Court's Last Full Week Is Its Fullest," July 4, 1976.

Lesley Oelsner, "Banned—but for How Long?" *New York Times*, July 2, 1972.

Lesley Oelsner, "Justices Uphold Death Penalty; Require Guidance for Imposing It, Limit Laws Making It Mandatory," *New York Times*, July 3, 1976.

Bill Rankin, "Fairness of the Death Penalty Is Still on Trial," *Atlanta Journal and Constitution*, June 29, 1997.

William Robbins, "Nixon Backs Death Penalty for Kidnapping, Hijacking," *New York Times*, June 30, 1972.

Tracy Thompson, "Once 'Unfit to Live,' Ex-Death-Row Inmates Winning Parole," *Atlanta Journal and Constitution*, March 12, 1987.

Tracy Thompson, "Who Shall Die? The Death Penalty's Last Appeal: Death Penalty Foes Girding for Final Supreme Court Battle," a five-part series, *Atlanta Journal and Constitution*, October 12–16, 1986.

James J. Tomkovicz, "The Endurance of the Felony-Murder Rule: A Study of the Forces That Shape Our Criminal Law," *Washington and Lee Law Review*, Fall 1994.

Eric Velasco, "New Lease on Life: Personal Growth, Luck Have Led Some from Death Row to Freedom," *Macon Telegraph*, July 13, 1995.

Warren Weaver Jr., "Death Penalty a 300-Year Issue in America," *New York Times*, July 3, 1976.

Websites

DeathPenalty.Net (deathpenalty.net). An informative anti–death penalty website maintained by organizations opposed to the death penalty. A good resource for current arguments against the death penalty.

The Oyez Project, Northwestern University (oyez.nwu.edu). After downloading a media player (with links provided at this website), one can listen to Supreme Court oral arguments in a number of significant cases, including *Furman v. Georgia*. Also provides a virtual tour of the Supreme Court building. Hear what Anthony Amsterdam, Dorothy Beasley, and the justices sounded like on that day decades ago.

Pro–death penalty.com (prodeathpenalty.com). An informative pro–death penalty website with links and statistics. It lists currently scheduled executions with descriptions of the crimes involved.

Index

Picture Credits

Cover photo: © Michael Schuman/SABA
© AFP/CORBIS, 94
AP Photo/Jack Smith, 9
AP/Wide World Photos, 19, 21, 24, 37, 45, 83
Archive Photos, 66, 69
Photograph by Joseph Bailey, National Geographic Society, Courtesy of the Supreme Court of the United States, 68
© Bettmann/CORBIS, 17, 20, 23, 31, 34, 43, 49, 51, 55, 73, 77, 81, 85, 86, 91
CNP/Archive Photos, 59
Peter Ehrenhaft, Collection of the Supreme Court of the United States, 60, 75
© Owen Franken/CORBIS, 15
Harris and Ewing, Collection of the Supreme Court of the United States, 46, 65
Hessler Studios, Collection of the Supreme Court of the United States, 62
© Hulton-Deutsch Collection/CORBIS, 33
Photograph by Joseph D. Lavenburg, National Geographic Society, Courtesy of the Supreme Court of the United States, 79
Library of Congress, 27, 29, 57
National Geographic, Collection of the Supreme Court of the United States, 71
From the Collections of the Supreme Court of the United States, 40
© Underwood & Underwood/CORBIS, 39
UPI/CORBIS-Bettmann, 13, 52

About the Author

Bradley Steffens is the author of eighteen nonfiction books for young adults, including *Free Speech* and *Censorship*. He lives in Poway, California, with his wife Angela.